COPY

MW00562601

For information, address Fred Helfers at helfers@arczip.com.

K9 Nose Work, Barn Hunt, Q-tips, Solo cups, and other products mentioned in this book are trademarks, service marks, and/or registered trademarks of their respective owners.

Jacket photographs by Sue Town of Pinnicle Photography

Jacket design and layout design by Cate Bramble

ISBN 978-0-996-1899-3-4

Permissions

Images in Figures 10, 48, and 50 by Sue Town of Pinnicle Photography.

Figures 1 – 6, 9, 18 and 19 by Lee Titus, Thin Blue Line K9 LLC.

Figures 7 and 8 by Craven, Brent A., Eric G. Paterson, Gary S. Settles, and Michael J. Lawson.

DEDICATION

To the detection dogs in my life:
Sammy, Corky, Lexi, Casey, and Jillie.

I strive to honor the lessons each taught me.

The Nose Work Handler: Foundation to Finesse

Fred Helfers

ACKNOWLEDGMENTS

Dr. Ken Furton — Florida International University. For introducing me to the science of canine olfaction, and his continued support and encouragement.

Ron Gaunt — Cofounder of the National Association of Canine Scent Work (NACSW). For 30 years of friendship and for introducing me to the wonderful world of K9 Nose Work.

Lee Titus — U.S. Customs (retired), Thin Blue Line K9 LLC.

Rudy Schimscha — Dog trainer for the Central Customs Authority of the Federal Republic of Germany. For sharing his wisdom and support during my early years in training detection dogs.

CONTENTS

THE POWER OF THE NOSE

I worked as a narcotics detective on investigations and handled drug dogs for more than 20 years. On one occasion, one of my partners was undercover buying large quantities of heroin from a known dealer. After the sale, our narcotics unit would continue surveillance of the drug dealer for future intelligence before making an arrest.

We observed that after drug deliveries the dealer regularly stopped at an out of the way, largely unused "park and ride" lot next to a nature preserve near the dealer's home. The dealer routinely walked into the nature preserve, stayed a few minutes, walked out, and drove home. We suspected that the drug dealer was using the nature preserve to hide drugs or money from the sale of drugs.

After the last drug delivery, the dealer did not stop at the park and ride — he went straight home. We were curious about what might be hidden in the brush. I decided to use Corky, my four-legged partner, to determine whether a hidden stash existed.

I knew from training and experience that the environment would dictate the type of application (search technique) to use with Corky. It was early December in the Pacific Northwest, around 8 PM, lightly raining, and around 40° F — in other words, it was cold, damp, and dark. Corky would need to get close to the source to detect any drug odor.

The nature preserve was an open area with several trails, probably 40 yards (36.5 meters) wide by 80 yards (73 meters) long. Tall grass and maple trees were surrounded by thick blackberry bushes which concealed the nature preserve from the road.

I positioned my human partners on the perimeter for officer safety. I put Corky on a 15-foot (4-meter) line, and started down-wind. Working a coal-black Labrador Retriever in the dark was a challenge. I couldn't use a flashlight because it would diminish our night vision and reveal our location. After approximately 15 minutes of Corky dragging me through blackberry bushes and under and over fallen trees, we approached a small stand of maple trees.

Corky was working hard, air-scenting into the light breeze. After showing no interest at the first maple tree, Corky approached the second. Just as she passed the tree Corky snapped her head to the side and buried her nose in the leaves that covered the ground.

The next thing I knew Corky was pelting me with leaves and dirt from her digging. Her change of behavior was so dramatic it surprised me, but her behavior was consistent with her training as an active-alert drug dog. That is, Corky was trained to dig at a source of odor.

I quickly pulled Corky away for her own safety. I didn't know if she had located drugs, the remains of a dead animal, or trash. I handed the leash to one of my partners and inspected the hole.

I should have trusted my dog! Approximately 18 inches (457 millimeters) underground I found a white plastic shopping bag. The bag contained more than half a kilo (more than a pound) of heroin.

My partners were amazed that Corky found the buried drugs and wanted to know how this was possible.

Several thoughts went through my mind. I suspected the dealer had recently disturbed the location. The soil was very loosely compacted, which would allow for odor molecules to readily work their way to the surface. The ground was covered with large maple leaves which worked like a blanket to trap the earth's heat and the odor molecules of the buried heroin. As Corky rapidly walked she was kicking up the fallen leaves and exposing the trapped odor.

Corky's find was the talk of the police department for days, and made me even more proud of my four-legged partner.

And now, science is beginning to understand the power of a dog's nose.

Chapter 1.
UNDERSTANDING OLFACTION AND ODOR

The focus in training detection dog teams is usually the dog. In reality, it is just as important to train handlers to become efficient, effective partners of dogs. During my three decades working with and training detection dogs and their handlers, it's apparent to me that people who want to excel at training and handling detection dogs must understand a dog's sense of smell.

Why Dogs Have Noses

Authors Pearsall and Verbruggen in their book *Scent: Training to Track, Search and Rescue* identify the following functions performed by the dog olfactory system.

- *Sense organ.* The nose is responsible for the sense of smell in a dog.
- *Airway.* The nose is part of the dog's respiratory (breathing) system.
- *Air conditioner.* Brings fresh air through and into the dog's respiratory system to help cool the dog.
- *Filter.* Helps to prevent impurities and foreign objects from entering the nasal cavity.
- *Origin of reflexes such as sneezing.* Expels foreign objects during sneezing.

- *Resonator or sound chamber.* Amplifies communication (barking and whining).

The last function identified by Pearsall and Verbruggen — and probably the most important function, if we are to understand how dogs detect odors — is the use of the nose as a direction finder. The nasal cavity is divided by the septum into sides. Each side can detect minute variations in the strength and intensity of odor molecules. The source of odor molecules can be determined by these variations in strength and intensity.

Scent and Smell

What is scent?

Dictionaries describe *scent* as "odor molecules that emanate from a substance or source and that affect the sense of smell." William Syrotuck in his marvelous book *Scent and the Scenting Dog* describes *scent* as "being a combination of odors." He then defines *odor* as "relating to a specific thing or object."

Throughout this book, when I use the word *odor*, I mean odor molecules that are emanating or coming from a specific source.

What is smell?

A *smell* is a perception by the sense of olfaction mediated by the olfactory nerve. Everything that you and a dog can perceive by olfaction emits molecules.

In general, molecules that can be smelled are:

- Lightweight (move in the air)

- Volatile (evaporate easily)

- Soluble (are broken down by moisture)

The Canine Olfactory System

Moisture and heat must be present for smelling (*olfaction*) to occur. Think of olfaction as an equation: olfaction = moisture + heat.

Odor molecules enter the nose and travel through the nasal passageway. As the air moves it is filtered, warmed, and humidified. Specialized receptor cells use *cilia* (hairlike projections) to capture odor molecules, as you see in Figure 1. The olfactory cilia send a signal to the olfactory lobe of the brain where odor is recognized, interpreted, and stored.

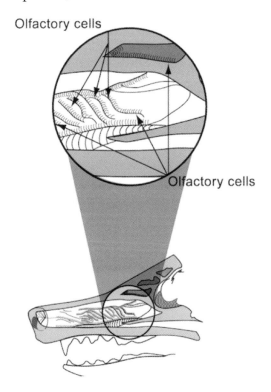

Figure 1 Olfactory cells, showing cilia

Because dogs need moisture in the nasal cavity to help process odor molecules, a lack of moisture can severely restrict scenting ability. When you work a dog in a dry, dusty environment or an environment with air conditioning, frequently inspect the dog's nose for dryness and ensure that the dog stays hydrated.

Turbinates

Turbinates are bony ridges covered in mucous that control air movement. A dog's nose contains *maxillo* (large) turbinates that create turbulence and begin heating and moistening the odor molecules. They are located in the front of the nasal chamber.

A dog's nose also contains *ethmo* (small) turbinates further back in the nasal chamber, where odor molecules spin faster and generate more heat. Ethmoturbinates have the greatest concentration of olfactory receptors. See Figure 2.

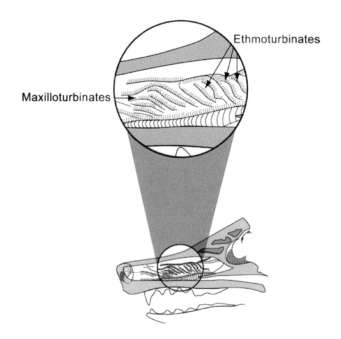

Figure 2 Turbinates: Maxilloturbinates (left) and ethmoturbinates (right)

Olfactory lobe

The olfactory lobe is where odor is recognized, interpreted, and stored in memory. See Figure 3.

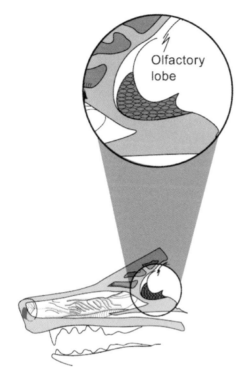

Figure 3 The olfactory lobe

Vomeronasal organ

Also known as the Jacobson's organ, the vomeronasal organ is a narrow tubular canal running behind the front part of the nose, behind the main canine tooth, and along the roof of the mouth, as in Figure 4. This organ contains olfactory cells and nerve bundles that connect to the olfactory lobe of the brain. The vomeronasal organ detects pheromones, primarily ones related to mating.

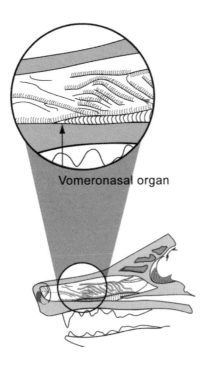

Figure 4 The vomeronasal organ

The position of the vomeronasal organ explains why keeping a dog's teeth healthy can help prevent infections that might affect the olfactory system and interfere with a dog's ability to detect odors.

Comparing the Human and Dog Olfactory Systems

When you compare the olfactory cell area of a human to a dog, you see that a dog has a large olfactory lobe and an elaborate nose design. A human's olfactory area is small and simple, as you see in Figures 5 and 6.

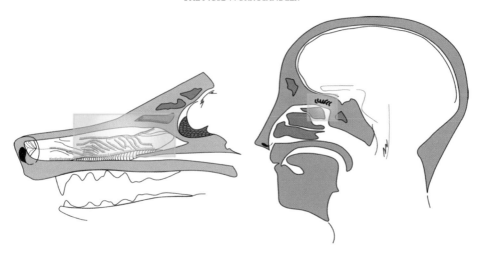

Figure 5 Comparing olfactory cell areas in dogs (left) and humans (right)

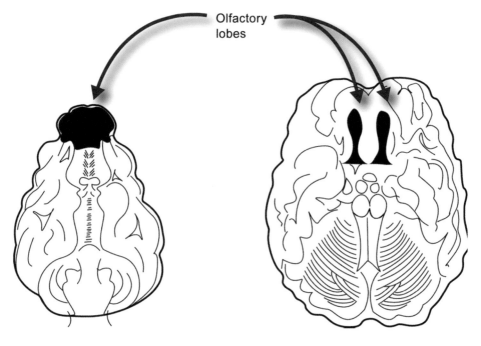

Figure 6 Comparison of olfactory lobes in dogs (left) and humans (right)

Humans have approximately five million olfactory sensory cells in their olfactory system. Large-breed dogs may have more than 200 million sensory cells in their olfactory system. However, a dog's ability to smell isn't related to its size. Smaller breeds and short-nosed (brachycephalic) dogs do not have inferior smelling abilities compared to larger breeds.

Anatomy of the dog nasal airway

Dr. Brent Craven and his associates Michael Lawson, Eric Paterson, and Gary Settles at Pennsylvania State University published an article that explains how odors move through a dog nose.

The researchers built a computer-generated model of the dog nasal airway. See Figure 7.

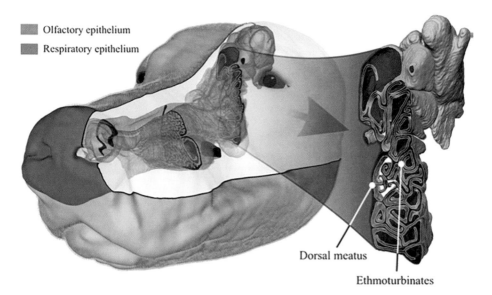

Figure 7 Computer-generated model of the dog nasal airway

Dog noses evolved two separate flow paths, one for respiration (breathing) and one for olfaction (smelling). Like the human nose, a dog's nose is divided by cartilage called the *septum*. The anatomy of a dog's nose enhances the dog's ability to smell.

During breathing, airflow takes a curved course up the middle of the nose and below the olfactory area.

Craven and his team state that when a dog breathes (see Figure 8), air bypasses the olfactory system:

> Airflow enters the nose at the left through the nasal vestibule. The red line indicates dorsal flow, the dark blue line indicates lateral flow, and the green line indicates ventral olfactory flow. The arrowheads represent the direction of airflow. (Craven, et al 2010)

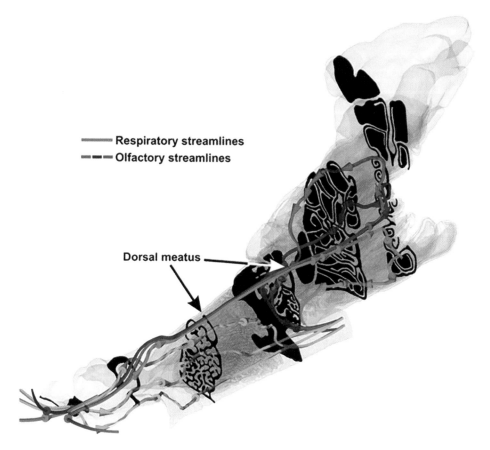

Figure 8 Airflow during respiration (breathing) and olfaction (sniffing)

Dogs *sniff* (perform a short, audible inhalation) to detect and identify odor molecules. Sniffing can occur as rapidly as three to five times a second. To better understand dog sniffing, researchers at the National Institutes of Standards and Technology (NIST) created a 3D-printed model of a dog nose. During sniffing, the dog uses sharp inhalation to pull the odor into the turbinates to help detect a particular odor. The odor molecules that reach the back of the olfactory recess are redirected 180 degrees through the ethmoturbinates. The additional time that molecules stay in the nasal cavity could be why dog noses work so well. See Figure 9.

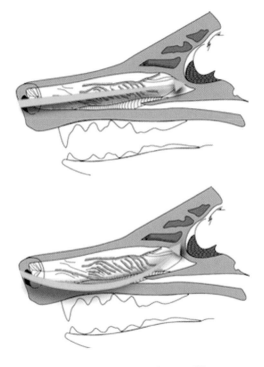

Figure 9 Airflow during sniffing

While a dog exhales through the slits at the side of the nose, new air is pulled in for processing. This process is called *active sniffing*.

Role of the alar fold

The alar fold, which is found just inside the dog nose, enables sniffing to occur with maximum effectiveness. See Figure 10.

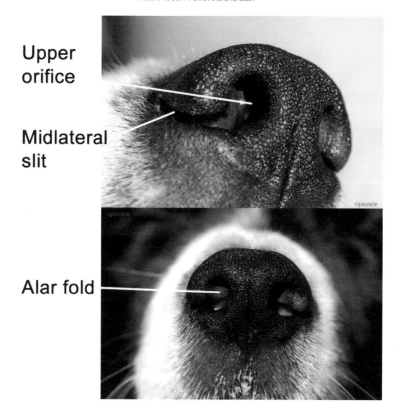

Upper orifice

Midlateral slit

Alar fold

Figure 10 Nasal anatomy, including the alar fold

Gary Settles explained in another paper how the alar fold works:

> When a dog inhales, the alar fold, a bulbous obstruction just inside the nostrils, opens to allow clear airflow through the upper part of the nose across the mucus-covered scent receptors. When air is exhaled, the alar fold closes off the top part and directs air down and out through the slits at the side of the dog's nose. This process creates a kind of suction that helps the dog inhale even more odor-laced air while also stirring up particles that might help deliver more scent. (Settles 2005)

Next, let's see how the dog olfactory system detects odors.

Scent Detection

Have you watched your dog running with its nose to the ground, apparently following an odor? Your dog's nose is working as a direction finder. I believe that a detection dog handler should understand how a dog's nose works as a direction finder.

Although dog nostrils are millimeters apart, dogs can detect an odor molecule at different times and strengths. When a dog encounters odor molecules that are stronger in one nostril, the stronger odor molecules attract (pull) the dog's attention in the direction of the stronger source. A dog will follow this odor source until the dog finds the odor source, loses the odor molecules, or detects that the odor molecules are weakening in strength. When the dog encounters a weakened source, the dog uses its nose to detect the direction of stronger odor molecules. You can see an example of this behavior in Figure 11.

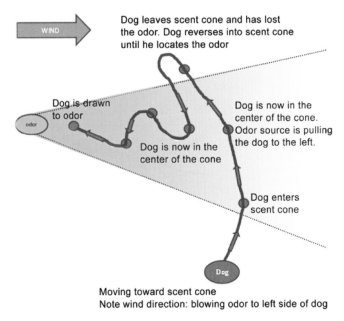

Figure 11 Example of a dog using a pattern to follow odor

A change of behavior occurs when a dog encounters or detects an odor source that the dog is trained to detect. The handler interprets the behavior change. I'll talk more about this important subject in Chapter 2.

Scent Picture

Scent picture can be defined as the combination of odors that are present when a detection dog identifies a *trained odor* (an odor that the dog is trained to detect).

Think about what you smell when you walk into a florist's shop. For a human, the smell of a florist's shop presents a scent picture.

When you want to apply (work) your dog, usually you look at the working area before you begin. For example, if you are going to search a classroom, you quickly look at all of the objects in the room. You might be overwhelmed by the objects — your dog isn't. A dog doesn't concentrate on the objects. At the threshold of the classroom, a dog uses its olfactory system to create a scent picture of the classroom.

A human version of a scent picture

Figure 12 shows an empty box. The odors that are present include those from the construction of the box (the cardboard, glue, odors from whoever handled the box, and so on).

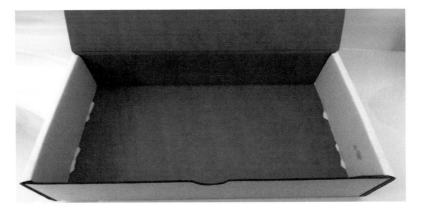

Figure 12 Scent picture of an empty box

Add an item such as a plastic container with treats to the box, as in Figure 13. Now the scent picture includes the odors of plastic and food.

Figure 13 Scent picture of a box with plastic container and food

Remove the container and the scent picture changes again (see Figure 14). Odor molecules remain from the missing container and food. This is called *residual odor.* More on residual odor in a bit.

Figure 14 Scent picture after the plastic container is removed: Odor molecules from container and food are still present

Scent Discrimination

Scent discrimination can be defined as the ability to locate and identify a trained odor when other odors are present.

Humans use this ability every day. People smell vegetables and fruit for freshness. Some smell milk in the fridge to decide whether it has gone bad. While you smell a rose in a florist's shop, the scents of the other flowers haven't disappeared. You simply aren't concentrating on them.

A dog uses scent discrimination at a level humans cannot achieve. For example, you might smell a freshly cooked cheeseburger — that's the extent of your scent picture. A dog creates a scent picture that can discriminate the meat, cheese, bun, tomato, lettuce, pickles, and condiments (see Figure 15).

Figure 15 Scent discrimination of a cheeseburger: Human (top), dog (bottom)

Consider how this ability to discriminate odors helps a dog that is trained to detect a drug such as cocaine. When the dog encounters cocaine odor molecules inside a coffee jar, the dog detects the odor molecules of coffee, cocaine, and whatever other odor molecules may be present. Because a drug detection dog is trained to give the handler an *alert* (a response in the presence of drug odor), when the dog performs its alert at the coffee jar the handler knows that drug odor is present.

Residual Odor

Residual odor can be defined as the odor that remains after the source of an odor is removed.

Everyone is familiar with the smell of burnt popcorn in a microwave. The popcorn was removed, but some odor molecules remain. Same with the residual odor of cigarette smoke. The odor permeates your clothing and remains long after the smoker leaves.

How long odor molecules will remain depends on factors such as temperature, humidity, length of exposure to odor, and the source of the molecules. When you apply your dog, remember that other odors are present and affect scent discrimination.

Factors that Influence Odor Molecules

Every detection discipline and sport encounters similar environmental influences, from fire scenes for accelerant detection dogs to the challenging environments of K9 Nose Work and Barn Hunt. Before we apply a dog we need to understand what affects odor and which influences are present.

The following factors influence odor molecules:

- The environment, including temperature, humidity, air movement (wind speed), and whether a search area is inside (interior) or outside (exterior).
- The quality and quantity of an odor source.
- Packaging and concealment of an odor source, such as buried sources.

Environment

What is the ambient temperature and humidity in the search area? Is the search area hot or cold? Is it raining? All these factors can assist or distract a dog searching for odor.

Temperature

Temperature and humidity affect odor by increasing molecular instability.

Heat

Heat affects odor. As air warms, an odor source expands and releases more odor molecules. Organic materials exposed to a warming environment — such as a sizzling steak on a grill — tend to release more molecules than chemicals like cocaine.

Cold

In cold environments, odor sources release few or no odor molecules. In general,

> Odor sources located in a warm environment allow the release of odor molecules more readily than those odor sources located in a cool environment. (Syrotuck 1972)

Humidity

Humidity is the amount of water vapor in air. The more moisture in the air (that is, the higher the humidity), the better the scenting conditions because there are more odor molecules present. Low humidity means that there is less moisture in the air and therefore fewer odor molecules.

Temperature and humidity together play an integral part in odor movement. The optimal scenting environment is moderate temperature and high humidity.

Hunting with my bird dogs in the early morning is generally more productive than hunting in late morning or early afternoon. Early in the morning, cool moist air tends to hold down odor molecules (in this case, from pheasants). Cooler air is more dense and holds more odor molecules. As temperatures rise during the day, the amount of humidity in the air declines along with the number of available odor molecules from an odor source.

Air movement

Slight breezes move odor in a way that might confuse a novice team, as you see in Figure 16. Applying a dog in a field when you don't understand air movement can be a frustrating experience.

Figure 16 Simulation of odor emanating from a box and moved by a breeze

The Scientific Working Group on Dog and Orthogonal detector Guidelines (SWGDOG) defines *scent cone* or *odor plume* as "a dispersion of odor in a given environment." Scent travels in the shape of a cone, and a scent cone moves with air currents. When strong or high winds encounter an odor source, the scent cone moving away from the source is long and narrow. When weak or low winds encounter an odor source the scent cone moving away from the source is short and broad, as you see in Figure 17.

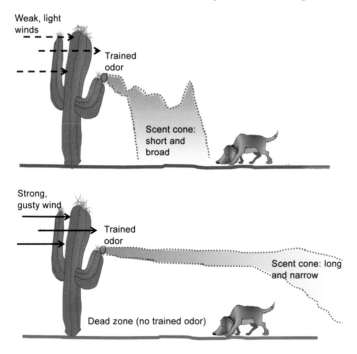

Figure 17 Scent travel in light wind (top) and strong wind (bottom)

Talk about being *upwind* or *downwind* is common in the world of detection dogs. In general, you are *upwind* when the wind is blowing toward a source of odor. For example, you are *upwind* if you are looking at a vehicle you are planning to search and the wind is hitting your back. You are said to be *downwind* when the wind is blowing away from a source of odor. For example, you are *downwind* if you are looking at a vehicle to search and the wind is hitting you in the face.

Obstacles and Air Movement

Wind that blows around and through obstacles redirects odor molecules around and over obstacles (see Figure 18). Redirection also occurs indoors, when air movement and obstacles are present. Air movements are affected by doorways, windows, bathroom vents, kitchen vents, forced-air ductwork, and floor vents.

Figure 18 Topography: Wind over hilly terrain

Figure 19 shows how a wind current moves odor from a source, hits the side of a hill, swirls, and rises over the top of the hill to create a *dead space* (an area devoid of a trained odor). Dead spaces can occur when odor molecules carried by a strong or turbulent breeze encounter physical objects (terrain, vegetation, or human construction). If a dog approaches from the downwind side and encounters a dead space, the dog can lose the odor source.

Figure 19 Topography: Wind over hilly terrain creates a dead space

Interiors and air movement

When you are indoors you usually have more control over temperature, wind, and the sources of other odors. You can manipulate the environment to provide the best scent picture for your dog by closing windows, managing heat, limiting air conditioning (because cool dry air can dry a dog's nose), and removing food sources. Train indoors at different times and at different locations so that your team gains experience in a variety of conditions.

Quality of an Odor Source

The quality of an odor source affects how many odor molecules are released. A pure substance releases more odor molecules than an adulterated or impure source.

Although other odor sources might be present, a dog should respond only to the odor that the dog has been trained to detect. If you train with essential oils, use only oils that have not been compromised or contaminated.

Quantity of an Odor Source

A more concentrated (intense) odor source contains more odor molecules. Train regularly using various amounts of an odor so that your dog can recognize odor molecules at different strengths. For example, use three to five Q-tips with odor for one drill, and use one or two Q-tips with odor for another drill.

Packaging and concealing an odor source

How you package odor to be searched — such as placing an odor in a tube or wrapping in plastic wrap — affects how odor is detected. It is the same for choosing where to hide an odor.

In basic classes for K9 Nose Work you learn how to handle tins, plastic tubes, and other containers to hold a training odor on a Q-tip. There are many ways to package odor for training or a competition, but everyone who packages and conceals hides for training or competition must have a working knowledge of odor. Someone who pays little or no attention to controlling the odor emanating from the odor source can prevent odor molecules from escaping in a timely manner for a dog to detect. This has disastrous consequences for dog teams.

Perhaps you want to hide odor inside the hollow metal leg of a chair, and plan to place the plastic end cap on the chair leg. This is an excellent concealment location, but you are increasing the difficulty of the search. You haven't allowed an easy escape route for the odor molecules. That hiding place may require hours, not minutes, for odor molecules to migrate and emanate from the chair leg. Leaving the end cap off the chair leg would give odor molecules a quick route to the outside and to a sniffing dog.

Wisdom from an Old Stove

In my early years of training detection dog teams, I used an old farmhouse for training several police drug dog teams. A couple of hours before the dog teams arrived, I concealed training aids (hides) throughout the farmhouse. The kitchen had a wood burning stove that wasn't being used. I decided to hide a quantity of heroin inside the stove, and I hid more heroin inside a metal tin on a shelf in the corner.

The six dog teams independently worked the kitchen "blind" (without any knowledge of how many hides or their placement). All teams easily found the drugs hidden on the shelf in the corner, but none of the dogs showed any interest in the stove. I was perplexed. These were experienced dog teams and the hide location was a simple exercise — or so I thought.

I inspected the wood stove. At first I couldn't imagine why the odor of the heroin wasn't escaping from the stove. Then it struck me: wood stoves are designed to allow air movement up the chimney. The flue to the chimney was open! This allowed any odor molecules escaping from the heroin to be sucked up the chimney. A simple trick using a match confirmed the movement of air inside the stove.

I closed the flue and waited a few minutes to allow the odor to move around the room. Again the dog teams searched the kitchen. This time, all six dog teams easily found the hide inside the stove.

Lesson learned. Always be aware of the effects on odor molecules when you place hides.

Buried Sources of Odor

Odor molecules from a buried source are affected by soil conditions. For example, the molecules of an odor source buried in soil move more quickly through a less-dense soil. Molecules migrate more slowly through and around denser soil, and eventually work their way to the surface.

The ground is usually warmer during the early evening as the ambient air temperature drops. The warmer ground enables odor molecules to dissipate and rise to the surface. Odor molecules generally stay close to the ground and may attach to dew or moisture.

While I was training a dog to detect natural gas leaks for a power company, it was not unusual for the dog to alert to the presence of gas odor molecules 15 to 20 feet away from a pipe buried 20 feet underground. The dog was locating natural gas leaks at a sensitivity level far higher than levels that pose a risk to humans. Spending thousands of dollars to excavate a pipe that leaks insignificant amounts of natural gas was not cost-effective. The project was shut down after approximately 18 months because the dog's nose was too accurate!

As you learn more about how odor moves and how dogs use their noses to find odor, your ability to apply a dog efficiently and successfully will improve. The handler drills in Chapter 3 will aid you.

Chapter 2.
READING YOUR DOG

Of the many questions that I have been asked in my years as a detection dog trainer, "How do I know when my dog has found a trained odor?" stands out. This question relates to learning to "read" or understand your dog — a skill that you can't acquire in a few simple sessions. It is learned throughout the life of your dog.

Reading your dog begins the moment when you bring home your four-legged companion. You observe your dog signaling "I need to go potty — NOW!" You understand "I really like this game!" as your puppy races throughout your house and yard in a fit of "zoomies." These common behaviors communicate a simple message.

During walks or hikes your dog displays its scenting abilities, but you are probably aware only when your dog sniffs a tree where another dog urinated. You will learn a great deal more about communication with your dog as you enter the wonderful world of scent games. The ability to read your dog will be defined by the scent games that you play, your interaction with your dog, and your ability to recall your dog's scenting behaviors.

I strongly recommend that you write down your observations (that is, keep a journal), and take videos of your dog as it encounters different odors in a scenting game.

Communication Formula

I believe that the key to reading a dog is less about observing the dog's behaviors when it finds a trained odor, and more about learning the behaviors your dog displays when it first encounters the scent cone of a trained odor.

The communication formula that I use and teach to detection dog handlers is Area alert (change of behavior) + Specific alert (final or trained response) = Alert. See Figure 20.

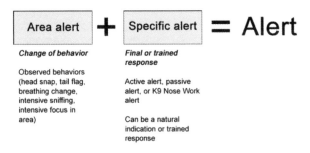

Figure 20 The communication formula

Let's look at each component of the formula.

Area Alert (Change of Behavior)

SWGDOG defines a *change of behavior* as

> A characteristic pattern of behaviors, as interpreted by the handler, that occurs when the dog detects a trained odor. This differs from other olfactory interests that otherwise are exhibited by the dog in response to the daily environment ... the pattern of behavior may be unique to each dog.

Examples of changes of behavior that you might have witnessed:

- Your dog stands on two legs to sniff something.

- Your dog crawls under tables or shelves to sniff something.

- Your dog sticks her head into small, tight places to sniff something.

A change of behavior is as unique as your dog. With training and experience you learn to read your dog's change of behavior.

I have seen reactions such as the following:

- Rigid body and intense focus
- Closed-mouth intense sniffing and "tail flag" (raised tail or tail arched over the dog's back)
- "Head snap" where the dog whips its head back and forth when the nose encounters a trained odor (see Figure 21).

Figure 21 Jillie demonstrates the head snap

Specific Alert
(Final or Trained Response)

The *indication* or *final response* is how a dog communicates that a trained odor is present. Whether the final response is sitting, staring, barking, lying down, or scratching depends on the training method.

In my experience, a dog's change of behavior is apparent to skilled handlers. However, novice handlers fixate on the final response. Novice handlers miss or overlook the change of behavior that the dog exhibits when detecting a trained odor.

When a dog cannot put its nose on an odor source there may not be a final response. In such situations the change of behavior is the alert, and that's how you should interpret the communication.

Rewarding Your Dog

I believe that there are two phases to rewards, *direct* (which includes pairing) and *alternate*. You move from the direct rewards to the alternate rewards as you train and your dog gains confidence in searching.

Direct Reward Phase (Pairing)

This phase is the most instinctive use of the dog's olfactory system and helps the dog become odor-obedient for a specific odor source with minimal handler intervention. The dog detects and goes to the source of the trained odor; then retrieves, eats, and/or plays with the odor source. The dog focuses on the odor source, and should stay with the odor source. See Figure 22.

Figure 22 Direct reward phase (pairing)

Alternate Reward Phase

In this phase the handler rewards the dog after the dog detects and goes to the source of the trained odor. The dog's focus shifts from the odor source, which previously provided the reward, to the handler presenting the reward as in Figure 23.

For example, in K9 Nose Work, a handler rewards the dog with food or a toy after the dog gives a final response to a trained odor.

The hazard in this phase is the possibility of a dog becoming handler-dependent.

A handler must continually train to speedily deliver a reward and minimize the risk of dependency in the dog.

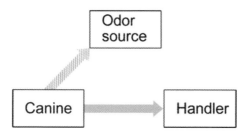

Figure 23 Alternate reward phase

Chapter 3.
LEASH HANDLING DRILLS

"Repetition is the mother of learning, the father of action, which makes it the architect of accomplishment."
— Zig Ziglar

You must build solid skills in basic dog handling to be an effective team member. This training starts early in the relationship with your dog, and increases in importance when your dog is introduced to trained odors. The skills in this chapter provide your team's foundation for effective searches.

Learning to Handle Leashes

This essential drill helps you learn to smoothly manage a leash of any length. Remember that the leash is a safety tool, not an instrument that you use to guide or direct.

1. Attach a ten- to fifteen-foot (three-to five-meter) leash to a chain-link fence at the approximate height of your dog's neck. See Figure 24.

Figure 24 Attach a leash to a chain-link fence

2. Walk to the end of the leash, keeping the leash off the ground as if you are trying to prevent your dog from becoming tangled. See Figure 25.

Figure 25 Walk to the end of the leash

3. Slowly walk toward the fence. Gather the leash in loops over the fingers of your left hand as you walk. Keep the leash off the ground, as in Figure 26.

Figure 26 Walk toward the fence

4. Stop when you reach the fence, then walk backwards away from the fence. Let the leash feed off your left hand. Keep the leash off the ground, as in Figure 27.

Figure 27 Walk backwards and let the leash feed off your hand

5. Repeat this drill several times. Increase and decrease your speed. See Figure 28.

Figure 28 Repeat the drill and vary your speed

Drills for Handling Dogs on Leash

The three leash-handling drills that I use in my basic classes —
straight-line, L-shape, and U-shape — help you to learn the
following skills:

- Presenting an application area or articles to a dog.

- Releasing the leash smoothly when the dog starts to search.

- Moving only after the dog begins searching.

- Keeping the dog focused on sniffing each object or area.

- Stepping to the side to traverse corners.

- Assisting the dog's progress.

- Turning and reapplying the dog.

- Rewarding the dog in a timely and consistent manner.

Straight-Line Drill

The straight-line drill is the first leash-handling drill that I teach, and it is the basis for all of the other drills. The drill uses six boxes, placed three or four feet (a meter or slightly more) apart in a straight line, as in Figure 29.

Figure 29 Example of a straight-line drill using Nosework Training Bowls

In the beginning you perform the straight-line drill by yourself, so that you become used to the movements — much like learning a dance routine.

Next, you perform the drill once or twice with your dog, but without using a trained odor. That way you can focus on your handling skills and not be distracted by your dog alerting you to a trained odor.

On the second pass of the boxes you will find your dog becoming more focused searching for an odor which you know is not present. The blank searches will build on your confidence in handling your dog.

Be sure to praise your dog for performing well during these "blank" searches (searches without odor).

Finally, you perform the straight-line drill with your dog and with a trained odor. (Dogs in the sport of K9 Nose Work are first trained to recognize a birch essential oil.)

It's helpful to use an assistant when you introduce trained odors. That way you can concentrate on learning to handle your dog. Someone else moves the trained odor to different locations, re-aligns boxes, and "pairs" odor boxes with treats (places treats as close as possible to the odor source, while making the treats accessible to the dog).

The following steps assume that you are performing the drill with your dog and with a trained odor.

1. Prepare a Nosework Training Bowl (see Figure 30).
    Nosework Training Bowls provide an effective tool to encourage a dog to stay at odor while being rewarded.

Figure 30 Example of a Nosework Training Bowl with the attached odor source

2. Place an odor source in the inaccessible vial at the bottom of the bowl (see Figure 31) and attach the vial to the bowl.

    The design of the bowl holds odor at the bottom of the bowl. The dog inhales the trained odor while it eats the treat. Your dog focuses inside the bowl while you reinforce the odor source with minimal distraction.

Figure 31 Odor Q-tips in the vial attached to the Nosework Training Bowl

3. Pair the odor source with a treat by dropping a treat in the bowl. The instant reward ensures that the dog does not become frustrated or what I call "box-happy" and tears, bites, or crushes the box to obtain the treat. The pairing technique occupies your dog until you arrive and reward the dog with another treat.

4. Place the boxes without odor in a straight line.

5. Have an assistant place the box with odor near the end of the line. For subsequent drills, the assistant can move the box with the odor at different places along the line.

6. Approach the starting position at the end of the row of boxes, approximately four to six feet (one to two meters) away from the boxes, so that the dog can create a scent picture (see

Figure 32). If you start the dog too close to the first box you won't have time to prepare yourself.

Figure 32 Start with the dog four to six feet away from the boxes

7. When you observe your dog sniffing or leaning into the search area, say your search command. As the dog moves, let the leash flow over your hand.

8. Give the dog time to sniff the first box before you move along with the dog (see Figure 33). Your goal is to enable the dog to search independently.

Figure 33 Give your dog time to sniff the first box

9. Let the dog sniff each box as you walk next to the line of boxes to keep the dog focused on the search pattern (see Figure 34). When you walk next to the line you unconsciously manipulate the dog to walk the pattern with you. Keep the hand with the leash above the dog's back, with the leash relaxed and loose.

Figure 34 Walk next to the line of boxes

10. Learn to anticipate what the dog will do at the last box in the line so that you can prepare to turn. Be prepared to turn with the dog as you reach the last box.

Turning with the dog

As the dog finishes inspecting the last box, take a few steps beyond the last box and change your handling side in front of the dog — some people call this a *front cross* or a 360-degree turn.

The goal is for the movement to be smooth and not interfere with the dog. Begin with a three- or four-foot (one meter) radius. A turn that is too tight will put you right on top of your dog and distract from the game.

Present the row of boxes to the dog once more without stopping (see Figure 35). The turn should be a flowing movement, with your team moving as one.

Figure 35 Presenting the boxes after the turn

Rewarding the dog

When the dog finds the box with the trained odor and eats the treat, you quickly reward the dog with more treats at the odor box (see Figure 36).

Figure 36 Example of how to reward at an odor box

The timing and placement of rewards are skills that must be mastered for your team's success.

When you know the location of a paired hide you can watch for your dog's reaction to odor. You have time to prepare yourself to reward the dog just as the dog finds the hide and eats the treat.

Do not wait until the dog finishes eating the treat. Move in immediately to reward at the location of the odor source (for example, inside the box with the odor). Your actions encourage the dog to keep its nose atop the odor source and to stay focused on the odor box, not on you.

Nosework Training Bowls make rewarding easier. The dog inhales a trained odor while eating the paired treat. You can quickly drop in a few more treats.

Crowding and Pushing

Avoid crowding or "pushing" a dog (moving closer so that you can quickly reward if needed). This (mostly unconscious) behavior is physical communication (body language) that affects your dog's scenting abilities by distracting from the game.

Novice handlers learn this behavior when they are told to reward quickly and "get in there and deliver the reward." When your team is first learning to search, standing nearby to reward quickly is an appropriate behavior for a handler. However, when your dog knows the basics of the game and is odor-obedient, you should be aware of your proximity and how your presence affects your dog.

When you observe your dog display a change of behavior in a search and your dog focuses on a hidden source, repeat to yourself: "As my dog goes in, I go out." Take a few steps away or backwards, allow the leash to flow over your hand, and give your dog the space he needs to work the scent pattern.

L-Shape Drill

This drill builds on the straight-line drill by introducing searches in corners (see Figure 37). The drill also boosts your confidence in moving while the dog searches.

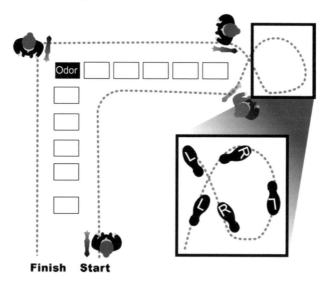

Odor

Finish   Start

Figure 37 Diagram of an L-shape drill

Perform one or two L-shape drills without odor, just as you did with the straight-line drill. Then have an assistant place a box with a paired odor source in the corner.

To perform this drill:

1. Start the dog just as you did for the straight-line drill. If you have been practicing, your dog will understand what to do. As the dog approaches the inside corner of the boxes, the dog should be a few paces ahead of you, on a loose leash.

2. Move your body so that, as the dog is sniffing the corner boxes, you continue moving along the the boxes. Your goal is

to move with the dog. Keep moving at a speed that does not distract the dog.

3. If the dog slows or stops to inspect a box, continue moving so that your body position does not indicate or suggest an interest in the box (see Figure 38).

Figure 38 Continue moving if the dog slows or stops to inspect a box

5. As you approach the end of the boxes, make a 180-degree turn to reverse the direction of your dog. This should be a fluid turn, because you don't want to use your leash to pull or correct the dog.

6. Present the boxes again.

7. When the dog finds the odor box and eats the treat, quickly reward the dog at the odor box.

Encourage your dog to search more by frequently moving the box with the odor source.

The "Box-Happy" Dog

During my basic training school with Sammy, we inspected numerous types of boxes and containers. Being an exuberant, high-drive, hard-working Labrador Retriever, Sammy embraced this task with gusto and was easily trained in detecting contraband. She thought that this game of detecting odors in packages and boxes was a lot of fun.

Part of Sammy's training was an active alert — biting and scratching at the source of odor. Sammy was encouraged to become more aggressive with her alert by vigorously scratching and also biting into the boxes that held odor. We were making Sammy fight for her reward. Due to my inexperience in handling and training detection dogs, I was training Sammy to become what professionals call "box-happy."

After basic training school, Sammy and I trained regularly with a U.S. Customs team from Seattle. Our teams trained weekly in a variety of search environments, including importation shipping facilities. We searched mail, packages, and shipping boxes.

I placed Sammy on a moving conveyor belt. She raced along the belt, biting into every box that she passed. I was embarrassed, shocked, and dismayed. I believed Sammy was a well-trained detection dog. From that experience I learned that my novice handling techniques had inadvertently taught Sammy to bite boxes whether not they contained a trained odor.

I needed to remedy the unwanted behavior. My U.S. Customs counterpart worked with me to train Sammy out of biting and jumping on every box.

We went back to basics. I reintroduced Sammy to straight-line searches of boxes on the ground. The first several drills used boxes without trained odor (that is, "blanks" or clean boxes). If Sammy showed an interest in any box, I said "Leave it!" and kept moving along the line of boxes. After several of these drills, Sammy showed no interest in blank boxes.

Next, my partner placed a box with a trained odor in the line of blank boxes. Sammy sniffed each box. When she found the box with the odor she displayed a change of behavior and final response. I rewarded her with her toy and praised her lavishly. These drills lasted fewer than ten minutes. At the end of each drill, Sammy received her toy reward and returned to her crate. Perhaps 15 or 20 minutes later I repeated the same set of drills. I did this three times a day for two days.

By the third day the unwanted behavior was gone. Sammy quickly and intensely inspected each package or box and gave her final response only at the ones that contained a trained odor. The next time that Sammy and I searched at the shipping facility it was a perfect day. Returning to basics worked for our team.

Your responsibility as the handler is to function as an impartial observer while your dog is searching. While you develop your skills you reward your dog quickly and consistently when they show a change of behavior at a trained odor.

Novice dogs can become frustrated if they aren't quickly rewarded. Frustration causes an aggressive response at a trained odor, such as jumping on, pushing, biting, and scratching. Pair a hide with a treat that is always and easily accessible to the dog. If the treat is not easily accessible to the dog, there is a likelihood of increased action and aggression in obtaining the treat, which in turn reinforces the unwanted behavior.

U-Shape Drill

Figure 39 Example of a U-shape drill

The goal of this drill is to give your dog access to each box in the corners, and to introduce an interior search pattern and an exterior search pattern (see Figures 39 and 40). The inside of the U becomes the interior perimeter of a room. The outside of the U becomes the exterior of a vehicle or another large object.

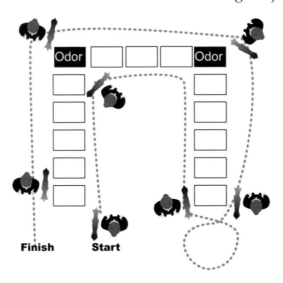

Figure 40 Diagram of a U-shape drill

Perform one or two U-shape drills without odor, just as you did with the straight-line drill and the L-shape drill. Then have an assistant place boxes with paired odor sources in the corners.

Do not be concerned if your dog misses a box or the corners. Usually the dog will inspect the boxes on the way back. With practice, your dog will slow down and sniff every box.

To perform this drill:

1. Start the dog just as you did for the straight-line and L-shape drills (see Figure 41). If you have been practicing, your dog will understand what to do. As the dog approaches the inside corner of the boxes, the dog should be a few paces ahead of you, on a loose leash.

Figure 41 U-shape drill: Starting the dog

2. Move your body so that, as the dog is sniffing the corner boxes, you continue moving along the second leg of the boxes and into the second corner. You move on the inside of the U-shape. This should be a fluid turn because you don't want to use the leash to pull or correct the dog (see Figure 42).

Figure 42 U-shape drill: Moving along the second leg of boxes

3. Keep moving at a speed that does not distract the dog. If the dog slows, or stops to inspect a box, keep moving so that your body does not influence a possibly false interest in a box (see Figure 43).

Figure 43 U-shape drill: Inspecting a box

4. As you approach the end of the inside U-shape, make a 180-degree turn to reverse the direction of your dog. After your team completes the turn, you are walking on the outside of the U-shape while your dog walks between you and the boxes. This should be a fluid turn because you don't want to use the leash to pull or correct the dog (see Figure 44).

Figure 44 U-shape drill: Example of turning at the end

5. Present the boxes again (see Figure 45).

Figure 45 U-shape drill: Presenting the boxes again

6. When the dog finds the odor box and eats the treat, reward the dog at the odor box (see Figure 46).

Figure 46 U-shape drill: Rewarding the dog

Encourage your dog to search more by frequently moving the box with the odor source.

Advanced Drills

Hanging Cups Drill

This exercise enhances your skills in leash handling and delivering rewards while your dog searches for a trained odor that is elevated and suspended. Your movements and the environmental conditions (air movement, temperature, and obstacles) affect the odor molecules in this drill.

Preparing the cups

Gather the following equipment:

- Multiple plastic cups, approximately 16 ounces (0.4 liter), such as Solo cups.

- Metal washers, approximately 1.25-inch diameter, and smaller washers. These provide weight in the wind and an attachment point for magnetized odor tins.

- A roll of twine or string.

- Magnetized odor tin, small and round.

Prepare all of the cups:

1. Poke a hole in the bottom of a cup.

2. Feed the twine through the hole in the cup.

3. Place large and small washers in the cup, and tie the twine to the smaller washer as you see in Figure 47.

Figure 47 Tying twine to washers

4. Measure and cut the twine. Consider a length that will enable you to tie the hide and adjust the height.

Stages

At first you perform this drill indoors in a room without air movement or breezes. When your dog is proficient at the different levels, you can move the drill outside.

Use one odor cup in your first drills. Place the magnetized odor tin on the washer at the bottom of the cup that will contain the trained odor (see Figure 48). For a paired hide smear a little peanut butter, cheese, or other food inside the rim of the cup.

Figure 48 Place the magnetized odor tin on the washer

Suspend one odor cup and the empty cups at the height of your dog's head (see Figure 49). Perform the drill in this configuration until your dog is proficient at finding a trained odor at that height.

Figure 49 Suspend the cups at the height of your dog's head

Use a long leash and let your dog work at a distance, as you see in Figure 50. Avoid placing yourself between the dog and the odor source.

Figure 50 Work your dog at a distance

Be patient. Your dog will need time to work the scent cone.

Gradually raise the height of the odor cups, but never higher than what your dog can reach on two legs, as in Figure 51.

Figure 51 Searching odor cups on two legs

As your dog gains confidence working odors at heights, you can gradually introduce more odor sources.

Eventually you can move the drill outside. Performing the drill outside is a new set of scenting problems that will require different levels of achievement like you used with the indoor drills.

Be patient. A breezy environment will make it difficult for your dog to quickly find the source until you have considerable practice at the game.

Minefield Drill

This drill challenges your handling skills and communication.

Preparing the minefield

Gather containers of various heights and sizes — everything from small containers to golf bags.

Place the containers inside a marked area that is approximately 20 feet (about 6 meters) wide and 30 feet (9 meters) long (see Figure 52).

Hide three or four odors in the containers, with at least two near or at the center of the search area. You should know where the hides were placed.

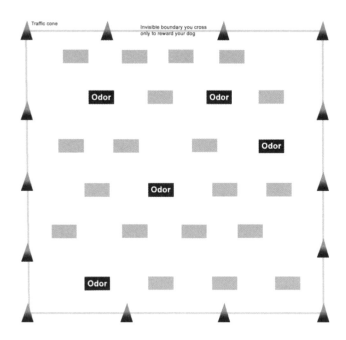

Figure 52 Diagram of the minefield drill

Use a long leash on the dog and start anywhere along the perimeter, as in Figure 53.

Figure 53 Searching the minefield

Walk outside the perimeter. Do not step into the search area until your dog alerts on a container. Move out of the search area after you reward your dog, and continue the search.

You can increase the complexity by performing this drill outside in a breezy area. Hide odors in elevated objects, such as in a box on a chair. This will require you to learn how to handle a leash above tall objects while your dog works.

Nosework Triangle Drill

This drill is for experienced dog teams with handlers that have shown confidence and repeated success in box drills. This is not a drill for beginners. It can be confusing and detrimental to a novice dog's progress.

This drill trains you to maximize your efficiency as a handler while you work with your dog as a team. At all times the dog faces into the wind and is given maximum opportunity to discover the scent cone for a hide, so it is a great drill for working through problems with converging odors.

Walk through this drill once or twice without your dog. Imagine that this is a dance around the vehicles. You stop, reward, and pivot each time your dog finds a trained odor.

Preparing the triangle

1. Position three vehicles four to five feet (at least a meter but not more than two) apart, with one vehicle perpendicular to the other two to make a U-shape as in Figure 54.

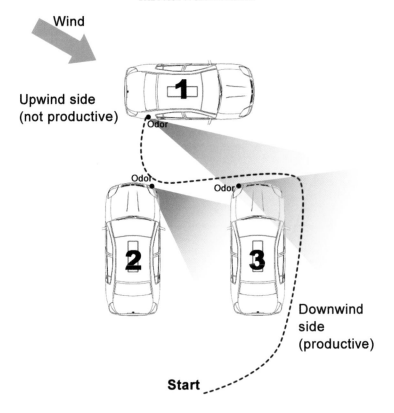

Figure 54 Diagram of the triangle drill

2. Prepare three containers of odor to hide on the vehicles. You can use the same odor for all of the vehicles, if you prefer. For example, if your dog is trained only for birch, prepare three odor containers with birch.

3. Determine the wind strength and direction. You want to place the hides so that the dog sniffs into the wind.

4. Place the odors in a triangular pattern:

   • *Vehicle 1:* Left front corner or wheel well, approximately a foot (a third of a meter) off the ground

   • *Vehicle 2:* Right front corner

   • *Vehicle 3:* Left front corner or wheel well

Performing the drill

1. Ready your dog at the start line. Notice the direction of the wind. In the example, the wind is blowing from the handler's left side.

   Look closely at Figure 54. Notice that the most productive area to apply your dog is in the triangular area between all three vehicles. Inside the triangle you can give your dog plenty of space to encounter a scent cone, and you can easily turn and present (what I call "open the door") to other scent cones.

2. Allow the dog to walk to the far downwind corner of the U-shape, immediately to your right and along the right side of vehicle 3.

3. Give the dog plenty of leash and space to sniff the downwind side and encounter the scent cone.

   As the dog goes to source you should be standing between vehicles 2 and 3.

4. As you reward your dog, pivot on your left foot approximately 90 degrees so that your body is facing vehicle 2 (see Figure 55).

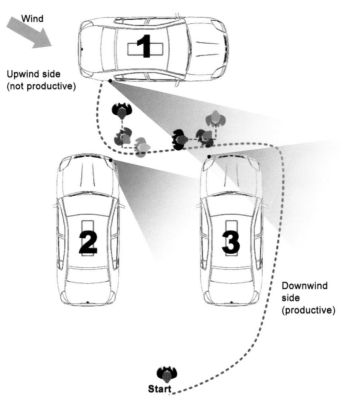

Figure 55 Triangle drill: Pivot to the next vehicle

5. Present vehicle 2 to the dog. The wind should be blowing odor to the dog.

6. Give the dog lots of leash to approach vehicle 2 and work the scent cone.

7. When the dog finds the source, reward the dog and move to the right side of the dog, between vehicle 2 and vehicle 1.

8. Pivot to face vehicle 1. Present vehicle 1 to the dog.

9. Give the dog plenty of leash and space to search vehicle 1 and find the odor source.

10. Reward the dog.

This drill requires your dog to work on a variety of scenting problems. The dog first encounters vehicle 3 at the most productive area to detect an odor, which is downwind. When the dog encounters the scent cone of vehicle 3 it is likely also encountering the scent cone from vehicle 1. Due to the wind strength and direction you may find that the scent cones of all three vehicles mingle or converge.

My experience shows that teams can effectively cover the three hides on three vehicles in well under 30 seconds. Although this is not a speed drill, the drill is designed to teach handlers confidence in moving from one object to another.

The techniques you learn in this drill can also be used for tight spaces, such as interiors with an alcove, a small lobby, or a small room next to a large room.

Y-Shape Drill

This drill is for experienced dog teams with handlers that have shown confidence and repeated success in straight-line, L-shape, and U-shape drills. This is not a drill for beginners. It can be confusing and detrimental to a novice dog's progress.

This drill builds skills beyond the basics (straight-line, L-shape, and U-shape). Your goal is to work each "leg" of the Y and transition from one leg to another without pulling the leash or heavily influencing the dog.

You will need a large indoor area to build the Y. Perform this drill inside first to minimize the influence of air movement.

Gather the following items:

- Six-foot leash.

- Three chairs, placed back to back in a triangular formation at the center of the Y (see Figure 56).

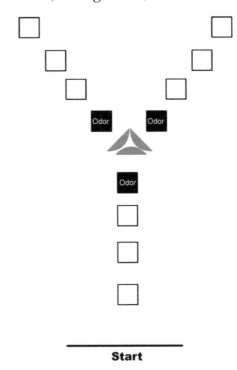

Start

Figure 56 Diagram of the Y-shape drill

- 12 Nosework Training Bowls, or boxes, or similar objects.

- A minimum of three prepared odor sources.

- An assistant.

Preparing the area

1. In front of each chair place four Nosework Training Bowls and/or boxes in a row.

   The boxes should be approximately four feet apart and lead away from the chairs, as you see in Figure 57.

Figure 57 Photograph of a Y-shape drill

2. Instruct the assistant to place a trained odor in the first box in front of each chair. Include a treat with each hide.

Performing the drill

1. Begin the drill like a straight-line search. When your dog reaches the paired hide near the chair, reward your dog.

2. Pivot to your right 45 degrees to face the next leg (see Figure 58).

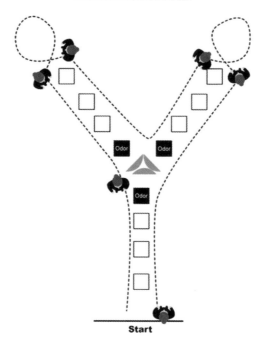

Figure 58 Diagram showing how to perform the Y- shape drill

3. Step forward and continue the search. Reward your dog when he finds the odor.

4. At the end of the row of boxes turn your dog (perform a front cross). While you move away from the odor boxes, your assistant quickly drops a treat into the bowl of the odor boxes. The assistant repeats this task while you work.

5. Reapply your dog to the leg you just worked, but on the opposite side. Reward your dog when he finds the odor.

6. Pivot to your right 45 degrees to face the next leg.

7. Step forward and continue the search. Reward your dog when he finds the odor.

8. At the end of the row of boxes turn your dog (perform a front cross).

9. Reapply your dog to the leg you just worked, but on the opposite side. Reward your dog when he finds the odor.

10. Pivot to your right 45 degrees to face the next leg.

11. Step forward and continue the search. Reward your dog when he finds the odor.

12. Pivot again and continue the search, or finish when you complete a circuit.

To increase the challenge, ask your assistant to move the boxes with the odor to different locations while you are working.

Moving the Y outdoors

When you achieve a consistent level of success performing the Y-shape drill indoors you can build the Y outdoors — with vehicles (see Figure 59).

Figure 59 Y-shape drill performed with vehicles

Place the odors so that you maximize the wind direction and create the potential for a converging odor challenge.

Work your dog just like you did on the indoors version. You will find that your handling skills are more fluid and confident.

Chapter 4.
SEARCHES AND SEARCH STRATEGIES

You learned how to handle your dog on the straight-line, L-shape, and U-shape exercises. You feel comfortable and confident in handling your dog. You are ready to develop a search strategy.

During detection dog training sessions, classes, conferences, and seminars, I am amazed how little knowledge most handlers display on the mechanics of working a dog in detection work. Most of the handlers that I meet are successful and competent — that isn't the issue. When I ask about their plan before applying the dog, or ask them to explain their actions while working with their canine partner, most say something like, "Well, I will just apply my dog and he will do the rest." They assume that their partner will intuitively understand the task. The handlers fail to realize that they affect how well their dog performs.

A search has the following components:

- Search plan and backup plan
- Safety check
- Environmental conditions
- The search itself

Search Plan

Every search must have a plan, which defines a course of action to accomplish an objective. For example, your goal could be to search a room and determine whether the room contains one or more odors. Your search plan would define your strategy to accomplish that goal. When you work with a plan and hold yourself accountable, your team can effectively and efficiently clear a search area.

A plan is typically based on your experience and your perception of the search area. A good plan helps you to define the search area before you start, maintains consistency, and allows flexibility when the dog tells you where the search should go based on the scent picture.

Planning for flexibility

What do you do when your dog disagrees with your search plan? Here's where the flexibility part is important. Allow the dog to investigate the area that first attracted the dog's attention. The dog knows the scent picture. There may be an odor that is attractive to the dog and you need to allow investigation. If the dog then shows little interest, redirect and reapply your dog to an area that you know you have just searched by overlapping at the point where the dog left the search plan.

For example, you are about to search a room. You decide at the threshold (doorway) that you will work the dog on leash, moving clockwise, because you know that a room is essentially the same as a U-shape drill. However, when you begin the search your dog has a different idea. She runs to a trash can in the center of the room, sniffs for a few seconds, loses interest, and starts wandering around the room. That's the time to reapply the dog at the threshold and start your clockwise search. You allowed the dog to sniff the trash can. The dog effectively "cleared" the trash can (communicated that no trained odor is present), and doesn't have to sniff the trash can again.

When my dog breaks my search plan I reapply the dog in the last area that we searched before the break. I overlap to ensure that I've covered everything.

Backup plan

You activate your backup plan when your dog experiences a negative situation during the search, fails to find the source of odor, or whenever there is no trained odor present — such as in a competition when one of the rooms to be searched does not contain an odor.

You want to achieve a supportive, positive outcome for your dog. Before your search, prepare a simple hide that enables your dog to be successful. At a K9 Nose Work trial you could use the recovery boxes, for example.

When I handled drug detection dogs and searched container shipping facilities, I would place a training hide somewhere outside of the search area — a neutral location, much like the recovery boxes. After working for twenty or thirty minutes, we left the search area for the neutral location and my dog found the training hide. Playing with her toy as a reward for finding the training hide reinforced the work and made her happy when a search was unsuccessful or upsetting.

Safety Check

A safety check is not the human version of a search for odor. It is your visual confirmation that you can apply your dog in a safe environment.

Your safety check could be a formal walk-through before a competition, or a visual inspection of an area where you plan to perform leash handling drills or other exercises. Perform the safety check as if you were working a dog.

This routine should sound familiar to people who participate in canine agility. A walk-through can build "muscle memory" of the search environment. In general, you will apply the dog in the same manner that you conducted the safety check to ensure that your team works consistently and does not overlook any areas.

Identify any hazards that could affect performance. Remove exposed chemicals and food when possible. If not, identify these as areas to avoid or that should remain outside a search area.

Pay particular attention to cabinets that store caustic cleaning agents, solvents, poisons, etc. Identify physical hazards such as slick floors, stairwells, low ceilings and rafters, plumbing fixtures, and electrical wiring. Be aware of other animals which may create a hazard for or distract your dog.

If you are working with an assistant or volunteer, ensure that they have some knowledge of detection dog searches. What may be "secure" to an inexperienced assistant could be a disaster for a search team.

Boas and Budgies

My human partner obtained a search warrant to look for drugs in a residence. I arrived a little later to work Sammy, my drug dog. I relied on my human partners to secure the area and conduct a safety check.

I went right to work with Sammy. After a few minutes spent clearing some rooms, we entered a back bedroom. The room was a mess: dirty clothes stacked in a corner, food debris on the nightstand — a regular pigsty.

I worked Sammy on leash, as usual, for safety. Sammy showed no interest in the food scraps. She immediately focused on the pile of dirty laundry. I noticed that the pile had started to move. I pulled Sammy away from the laundry pile just as the head of a boa constrictor emerged.

The boa was roughly six feet long and seemed agitated that Sammy had disturbed his resting spot. I was upset that the room hadn't been checked for dog and handler safety. But I was to blame, because the safety check was my responsibility.

Sammy and I got our revenge. When I told my partner (who was responsible for securing the area) that we found something in the bedroom, he raced in the room only to be greeted by the boa just inside the door. I knew that he was afraid of snakes.

On another occasion while searching a drug house for cocaine, I started working Sammy without conducting a full safety check.

We entered a small bedroom and I noticed some movement off to my right. Sammy possessed the better detection skills. In one great leap she started climbing the curtains. The curtains, rod, and all crashed to the floor as two parakeets frantically tried to escape Sammy's eager jaws.

The birds survived. Sammy instilled in me the need to conduct a safety check.

Environmental Conditions

As I explained in Chapter 1, environmental conditions can be very frustrating if you fail to consider how air flow, air conditioning, temperature, humidity, etc., might affect your search plan. For example, if you are unaware of a heat source you can become confused and misread your dog.

Before a search

Your routine before a search is just as important as what you do during a search. I call this a "presearch routine."

As you approach a search area, identify any changes that might have occurred since your walk-through. Review the environmental conditions.

Your mindset

Your frame of mind plays a very important role. Handlers are notoriously nervous before applying their dogs. This is especially true when you don't know where odor is hidden.

Your opinions about the search area are formed at the same time that the dog forms a scent picture. Keep in mind that what you think is important may not be important to your dog.

The pressure or stress in your mind can be used to your advantage. Take time as you are approaching the start line or the threshold. Revisit the positive aspects of handling your dog. The many hours you have spent working on your handler drills have reinforced your ability to read and trust your dog. Never underestimate your ability to read your dog!

For example, as you are approaching a vehicle, think about how your team has trained many, many times for just this situation. Think how often your dog has successfully found the odor source. This self-talk builds your confidence. Trust your dog and the outcome will be positive.

Think of three letters — MRP — as you are getting ready to search.

M stands for *mental image.* You visualize how you will successfully handle your dog through a search.

R stands for *relax.* Train yourself to become more composed and less tense. Composure and relaxation communicate confidence to your dog.

P stands for *patience.* Give your dog time to create the scent picture in the search environment.

Search commands

The one aspect of the training session that should be automatic is the search command that tells your dog to begin the game.

A search command can be simple — "Search!" or "Find it!" — or something unique that the dog recognizes. One K9 Nose Work competitor I know uses the command "Rock 'n' roll!" The team's enthusiasm is impressive.

Establish a command for your dog and join in the fun.

During a Search

Obstacles

When you search indoors you are likely to encounter physical barriers such as furniture. Most handlers will attempt to apply their dog without moving furniture, although the furniture interferes with the dog. That's because manipulating a strange environment is not socially acceptable and makes some people uncomfortable. At K9 Nose Work competitions, you may be required to request permission from the judge before you move anything.

An experienced handler thinks about accommodating the dog, and that may mean moving furniture, stepping on furniture, or walking over or under furniture. You must allow your dog the opportunity to investigate all areas. After you move an object the dog can inspect the new area and the moved object for a more thorough search.

Alert!

When the dog alerts you to the presence of a trained odor, take a few seconds to reward and praise your dog, and then continue.

End of the search

Many handlers turn and walk away at the end of a search. This can be a mistake. As you finish the search, stop for a few seconds where the search began. Quickly look over all of the areas where you applied your dog. Follow the direction or pattern you used in your search. This may help you to recall areas your dog missed or demonstrated an interest.

Release the Hounds!

Let's look a vehicle search with Sandi and her dog Haley. Sandi knows that a vehicle search is like a leash-handling drill she's performed many times. Sandi already performed a safety check and created a search plan. Team Haley is ready.

Where possible, start downwind so your dog can quickly build a scent picture with odor molecules carried from the vehicle. Team Haley chose the downwind side, shown in Figure 60.

Figure 60 Vehicle search: Near the start line, and downwind

Depending on wind strength, and whether the situation permits (such as the positioning of a start line), apply your dog six to eight feet (1 to 2.5 meters) from the end of the vehicle. See Figure 61.

Figure 61 Vehicle search: Crossing the start line

I train handlers to move counterclockwise around a vehicle because most people train their dogs to heel at the left side (see Figure 62). This method ensures that your dog will be between you and the vehicle, or somewhat ahead of you. You are less likely to interfere with the dog or block the dog from finding an odor source on a vehicle.

Figure 62 Vehicle search: Following Haley

The exception to this advice occurs when a handler gives the search command and the dog immediately displays a change of behavior, as in Figure 63. In other words, strive to be flexible and to be prepared to adapt the search plan based on what the dog is telling you.

Figure 63 Vehicle search: Haley has a change of behavior

Haley doesn't walk along the side of the vehicle as Sandi planned. Instead, Haley runs to the rear of the vehicle and intensely sniffs the trunk seam.

The change of behavior indicates that Halley followed an odor to its source. Sandi didn't need to give her search command again because Sandi observed the change of behavior — repeating a command may distract the dog.

When Haley inspected the rear of the car and showed no further interest, Sandi continued following her search plan by moving the team counterclockwise around the vehicle. Sandi allowed Haley to further inspect the exterior of the vehicle.

As Haley closely inspected the exterior of the vehicle and displayed no further change of behavior — and Sandi felt comfortable with the search (trusted her dog) — then Sandi ended the search.

What would have happened if Sandi noticed Haley displaying a strong interest in another area of the vehicle? Sandi would give Haley access to that area for inspection (sniffing), provide a lot of leash and complete freedom of movement. She would be thinking about not focusing on a specific area, so that she is not trying to convince her dog to respond.

Figure 64 shows a search like Team Haley's.

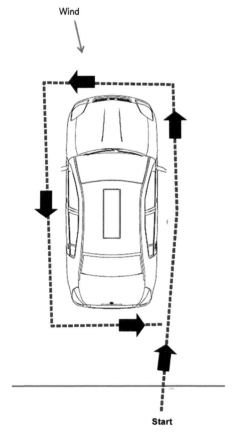

Figure 64 Single vehicle search counterclockwise

Search Strategies

There will always be odor influences that humans cannot detect. Your dog will tell you whether trained odor is present.

Searching Multiple Vehicles

Most handlers are overwhelmed by multiple vehicle searches because they immediately focus on all of the vehicles.

The fact that there are multiple vehicles to search means little to your dog. The vehicles are simply part of the scent picture.

Look at Figure 65. Analyze the wind direction from the front of the vehicles to the rear. The figure shows that the scent cone is flowing away from the vehicles.

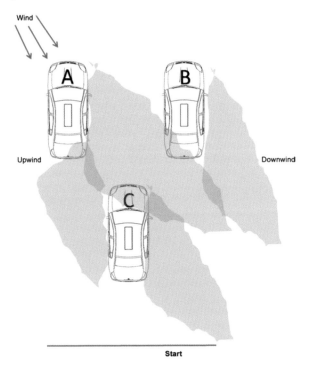

Figure 65 Example of productive search areas for a three-vehicle search

Look at the potential for productive areas (shaded areas) where odor from more than one vehicle is mingling. In the figure you see that the most productive area to search is in the loose triangle formed by the three vehicles.

Apply the dog on the downwind side of vehicle C, at the right tail light. Work counterclockwise and cover all three vehicles.

Figure 66 shows a diagram of a search pattern for multiple vehicles.

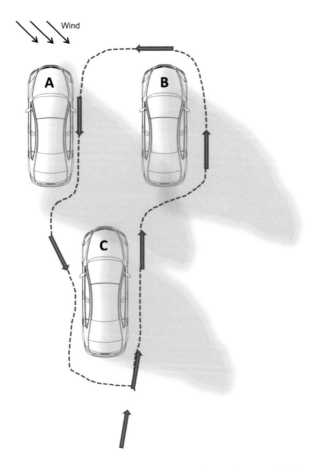

Figure 66 Example of a search pattern for a three-vehicle search

On-Leash or Off-Leash?

I strongly recommend that new handlers wait to work their dogs off-leash until they are proficient and confident in handling their dogs on-leash. Off-leash handling requires strong, subtle communication between handler and dog — communication that develops only after many hours of training. It takes a skilled, dedicated handler to correctly apply a dog off-leash as if the dog is working on-leash.

The following table provides some suggestions on leash use.

Situation	On-Leash or Off-Leash?
Dangerous search locations (moving traffic, on or near elevated areas, unstable footing areas, chemicals present, etc.)	On
Presence of animals, children, disabled, and/or elderly	On
Large areas	Depends on safety and training
Multiple searches for long periods	On
Safe areas with few or no hazards (no potential for the dog to run away, or dog has trained recall)	Off

A general strategy when working outdoors and off-leash is to start downwind and work your dog into the wind. If the start area or start line is upwind, quickly move your dog downwind so that the dog can use the wind to detect trained odors. Remember to use a search pattern.

For interior searches, first train in a room that is empty except for one or two pieces of furniture. Remember to use a search pattern similar to the ones you use when you work on-leash.

Off-leash applications can enhance a detection team's capabilities in small rooms, open fields, and vehicles, but you must always remember the safety of your dog. Never apply your dog off-leash where the area may not be totally safe.

Presenting (detailing)

Presenting an area *(detailing,* in professional jargon) means that you direct a dog to inspect a specific area, such as seams and other areas where odors might be escaping. Handlers should not control or dominate the dog's natural ability to locate an odor source.

When conducted correctly, detailing is a team effort, as you see in Figure 67. When conducted incorrectly, detailing becomes a handler error. I will explain the error in Chapter 7.

Figure 67 Deputy Darin Boyd and Nelson detail a vehicle

Search patterns

A search pattern is a method of effectively covering an area while giving a dog an opportunity to inspect every part of the area. A search pattern uses a dog's olfactory talents in the most efficient, systematic manner. Patterns should not interfere with a dog's ability to work a scent cone.

Quartering

A quartering pattern helps to effectively cover large areas (warehouses, cluttered rooms, big fields). If you are outdoors, quartering works best when you are into the wind. See Figure 68.

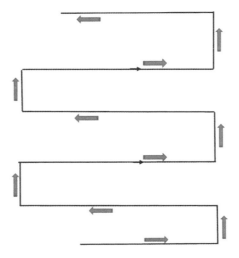

Figure 68 Diagram of a quartering pattern

Serpentine

Serpentine, shown in Figure 69, is a curving or winding pattern throughout a search area that enables a dog to access the entire area. You assist the dog by working downwind.

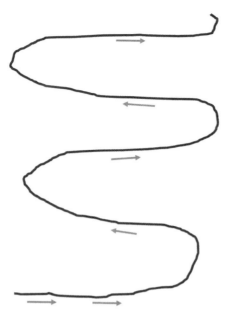

Figure 69 Diagram of a serpentine pattern

Spiral

A spiral pattern starts at the threshold of a search area and moves clockwise toward the center, as shown in Figure 70. A spiral pattern can be useful in a large interior space that does not have many obstacles.

Figure 70 Diagram of a concentric (spiral) pattern

Using search patterns indoors

Allow several seconds for the dog to develop a scent picture. While your dog is developing the scent picture, you identify somewhere in the room to begin and end the search — what I call a "point of beginning" or POB. A POB works as a reference point so you know where you have searched and where you still need to search.

Your POB may be determined by start lines in a competition, so you incorporate that information into your search plan. Finish your search at the POB to ensure that the dog searches the entire room and does not miss a trained odor.

You can apply the dog clockwise from the start line or perimeter. Because interiors are not simple, you may need to apply the dog in a spiral, quartering, serpentine — or all three.

Large areas of walls with shelves or lockers may demand a serpentine pattern so the dog is effective with minimal effort.

Work toward the center of the room. The dog will recognize its search parameters, build intensity and confidence, and increase interest. Help the dog play the game to increase your success.

Chapter 5. YOUR TRAINING PROGRAM

Training a dog to detect an odor in all environments begins with introducing your dog to those environments and ensuring the dog is comfortable, confident, and capable in those environments before training. Too often I find that detection dog training programs are designed solely for the dog and do not consider the training needs of the handler.

Sadie

In my early days of training drug detection dogs at my property in the state of Washington, I trained a young yellow Labrador to detect drugs. Her name was Sadie.

Sadie was a year old, impressionable, and had a fire in her to retrieve. She came from a gun dog kennel with a reputation for quality dogs. Sadie excelled at detection training on my property and quickly identified the odors of controlled substances.

One day I thought it was time to conduct some training at a nearby truck stop. The noise, strong diesel smells, and commotion of tractor trailer rigs coming and going was the perfect place to train Sadie in a new environment. I loaded Sadie into my pickup and off we went.

I parked away from the busy trucks and got Sadie out of her travel crate. Immediately I noticed a change in her behavior. A driven, confident, and intense retriever turned into a subdued, quiet, and skittish dog. What happened — was she sick? Did I do something wrong? My confidence in her was deteriorating as quickly as Sadie's confidence in me.

My lack of training experience was on display and Sadie was responding to my behavior.

Due to my training inexperience, I failed to recognize a basic tenet of educating young dogs: socialization of new environments. Before coming to me Sadie lived on acreage, training to hunt and retrieve birds. Yes, she excelled at the new game on my property and was impressive in her quick and natural desire to learn and please me. However, Sadie had never been exposed to *such a harsh and unnatural environment as a truck stop. It was an important lesson for me as a trainer. Training new dogs in new and ever-changing environments soon became my training regime. Sadie soon overcame this lack of confidence in new environments. As her confidence grew, so did mine. It was now a team effort.*

Sadie graduated and became a very successful drug detection dog for a police department in eastern Washington.

Training Philosophy

You and your dog are a team. Teams that do not have an established training program will experience performance problems. Weekly training sessions enable your dog to perform at an acceptable level while you learn to recognize changes of behavior in the dog. You grow as a team in your ability to detect trained odors.

I strongly urge every dog handler to build a training philosophy and to continue to review that philosophy over their journey with their dog. That training philosophy begins with a training program that is tailored to meet the needs of the dog and the shared activity. The philosophy includes realistic expectations on your part. We know that every dog is different — different needs, socialization, skills, life experiences, and so on. Your philosophy will be shaped in many ways, much like your dog.

My philosophy began in the late 1970s with hunting dogs. After many years of training professional detection dogs and handlers, and then being introduced to the civilian world of K9 Nose Work, my philosophy has changed dramatically and is still evolving.

Training a dog can be highly rewarding for a handler — and sometimes just as frustrating. Use positive reinforcement to achieve results. You present a motivating item (like a food treat or toy) to your dog after the dog exhibits a desired behavior. Rewarding the appropriate behavior makes the behavior likely to happen in the future. Positive reinforcement can be a powerful and effective method to shape and change behavior.

The following table explains some realistic goals of a training philosophy.

Goals for the Dog	Goals for the Handler
Scent discrimination: Repetitive, consistent training with continual exposure to a variety of trained odors. Scent discrimination builds on basic training and reinforces a positive response to trained odors.	**Reading your dog:** Learning the behavior changes that your dog demonstrates when encountering a trained odor. Consistent, regular training enables you to read your dog's characteristic changes of behavior. Your dog shows a distinct change of behavior when trained odors are present. This could be tail flagging, intensive sniffing, change of breathing, change of focus, or increasingly intense searching.
Introducing new areas: Familiarize your dog with searches in novel environments (slick floors, elevated hides, working off the ground, loud noises, distractions, etc.) so that the dog can overcome any apprehensions.	**Introducing new areas:** Working as a team in novel environments, such as supermarket parking lots, inside schools, or at busy parks gives you a chance to observe your dog under varying conditions. Familiarizing dogs with new areas builds team proficiency. Based on my experience, the dog teams that encounter the most problems are the ones that conduct minimal training and do not vary their training scenarios or sites. If you cannot demonstrate to your dog that you are confident in varying environments, your dog will sense this and become less effective when searching. Lack of confidence leads to a decline in performance.

Goals for the Dog	Goals for the Handler
Increasing confidence: A confident, self-assured dog displays those traits when working. Consequently the dog will be more successful in locating trained odors. Training sessions should focus on situations when the dog may show a lack of confidence or seems disturbed when working in new environments.	**Increasing confidence:** You work to build your team's confidence.When a handler displays a lack of confidence, the dog senses this and can become distracted. A dog that regularly works with their handler soon learns to read the handler, and the handler learns to read the dog.
Training regularly: Regular training increases your dog's scent stamina (the length of time that a dog can perform a scenting task). Build scent stamina to increase confidence that a dog can work scent problems for longer periods.	**Reinforcing training:** An established training program focuses on the basic training of the dog and reinforces your training philosophy. Reinforcement of positive rewards enables the dog to learn more rapidly and retain the training.

Bus Search

I went with my first drug dog, Sammy, to a border entry point to search a commercial tour bus for U.S. Customs. The driver had allegedly been smuggling cocaine from Canada.

Upon arrival I was unsure how to effectively work my dog because I had never trained on a large bus. Sammy could sense this lack of confidence. The result was a sloppy search of the interior and exterior of the bus.

No controlled substances were detected and I really felt uncomfortable about the search. (We learned later that the bus did not have any contraband.)

When I returned to my office I found a training site for working with our city buses, and eventually was able to sharpen my skills handling my dog on buses. As the training progressed, I could see that the confidence I displayed was "going down the leash." Sammy and I were working as a team.

THE NOSE WORK HANDLER

Education and Experimentation

I have seen a detection dog handler complete a training class and then let their handling skills stagnate. To continue the growth of a detection team you must expand your team's knowledge in all facets of detection dog handling.

Attend annual training seminars on detection work, train regularly with certified instructors, and volunteer at detection dog trials. Attend camps and seminars. Expand your knowledge of olfactory and scent topics by reading books and research papers.

As you train, work with a certified instructor to experiment with different scenting problems and handling situations. Introduce your dog to searches in new environments to build your team's confidence.

Resolve to answer questions like "Why is my dog behaving like this, in this environment? What is affecting the sources of odor?" Answering these questions increases your knowledge and skill in handling your dog.

How Often to Train?

Consider the science of dog olfaction. Every olfactory neuron has several cilia with receptors. These neurons live for 30 to 60 days and are then replaced by new neurons.

The receptor for a neuron (such as an olfactory neuron) is determined during the creation of the neuron. If an olfactory receptor for a specific odor dies, the replacement neuron may not contain the same receptor. Studies show that the determination of the new receptor is created to some extent by what the dog is frequently smelling. Dogs that consistently train on certain odors will develop more receptors for these odors.

In other words, science says that you can optimize your dog's olfactory system by participating in regular scent training. Training helps you, too, because you cannot become proficient in handling a detection dog unless you train regularly.

SWGDOG recommends that professional dog teams train at least 16 hours a month. If you want to compete in K9 Nose Work you should train weekly with a Certified Nose Work Instructor (CNWI). To reach a truly competitive level you may need to train four to six times a week. That does not mean implementing a rigorous training schedule such as one used by professionals. Training to that level may be destructive and a disservice to you and your dog. Rather, establish training with an educational goal. The exercises should last perhaps five or ten minutes. Vary the location, and emphasize the fun.

Training Suggestions

The routine weekly chore of grocery shopping can now become a training opportunity. Park in an area away from the store, place an odor source (training aid) in a safe area away from traffic. Keep dog safety, local laws etc., in mind when leaving dogs in vehicles.

Complete your shopping and put the groceries in your vehicle. Get your dog out of the vehicle and work that odor.

To your dog it is always a blind search. Your dog will experience a new environment, you will observe your dog's change of behavior in that new environment, and — most importantly — your dog will be successful in a training session.

If you take your dog on daily walks, vary your route. Before you walk, place the training hide along the route that you plan to take. You can pair a food reward with the hide. As you are walking your dog, be aware when the dog appears to detect the trained odor (that is, watch for the change of behavior). If your dog is not expecting this find, you will be amazed at the intensity your dog displays.

You might want to use a long leash so that the dog has freedom to go to source when the odor is discovered.

Above all, have fun!

Chapter 6.
RECORDKEEPING

Documenting skill proficiency has a lasting effect. That's why creating a journal to document your training is a good idea. A journal is not a diary. A journal documents how your team trains and competes, and includes the following information:

- Goal of a training session
- How often you train
- The odors you use in training
- The drills that you perform
- Where you train
- When you train
- How long you train
- The outcome of a training session (what worked, what didn't)

I use performance sheets, performance diagrams, and exercise logs in my recordkeeping. You can purchase a bound copy of a performance journal on my website *(fredhelfers.com)*.

The Performance Log

A performance log enables you to quickly document the details of training sessions.

A performance log should contain the following sections:

- *Date and time of drill.* Write in the date and time the drill was performed and note the duration of the training session.

- *Odor.* Write in the training aids (odor sources) that were used in the session.

- *Location.* Identify the physical location where the dog was worked.

- *Type of drill.* Identify the elements, such as vehicles or containers.

- *Whether the hide was known to the handler.* Did you know where the odor source was located?

- *Distractions.* Were there distraction odors present? Were toys or food placed in the search area?

- *Whether the hide was paired with a reward.* Did you supply a treat with the hide?

- *Number of aids.* Note how many hides were used for the drill.

- *Weather, temperature, wind, and light conditions.* A concise record of environmental conditions helps you to accurately evaluate scenting conditions.

- *Narrative.* A brief description of the training drill, including your observations of the dog's change of behavior at a trained odor source. You can describe how the dog was applied, including physical barriers to the dog that affected going to the odor source.

- *Team goals.* Identify at least one goal for a training session, such as "Improve handling my dog on a long leash." Set goals that are realistic and attainable for the session. Later you can measure your progress by reviewing the completed performance logs.

See Figure 71.

Nosework Dog Performance Sheet (exterior example)

Exercise # 3

Date *April 20th, 2014* / Time of exercise (duration) *3 minutes, plus 20 minute set up time.*

Dogs Name: *Corky.* Handler: *Fred*

Training Odors:e.g. Essential Oils (Birch) Clove (Anise)

Other _____

Location of exercise: *Children's Park, Tucson Arizona*

Type of exercise: (Dog application) Vehicles / Containers / (Exterior) / Interior.

Location of aids known to handler? Yes / (No) Distraction aids: *none*

"Paired" Aid? Yes / (No) Number of aids:_____2_____

Weather: *Sunny* Temperature: *75* f*

Wind: *light* Light : *Sunshine*

Team Goals: (What do you want to accomplish with your dog?)

To feel more comfortable allowing Corky to use her hunt drive! These exercises allow me to learn to trust my dog! Note: Do more off leash drills where it is a protected area!

Narrative: (Handlers observation and remarks of dog application)

Corky was applied on leash to an exterior exercise of a playground picnic area. With a command to "find it " Corky ran quickly in to the playground area. Working on a 15' leash. allowed Corky to work the wind that was blowing across the playground. Corky sniffed the b of a tree then left the tree and gave a COB by holding her head up high and sniffing into the wind. Corky then ran rapidly over to a picnic table. Corky stuck her head under the table top and then gave a sit response. I then rewarded Corky at source (under table top). I then direc Corky to the downwind side of the picnic table. Showing no interest I allowed Corky to the downwind side of the playground and around the swing set. Upon reaching the downwind si of the swing set I noticed Corky pick her head up and started sniffing intensely. Corky starte run towards the picnic table but when passing the leg of the swing set gave a COB by a heac snap and sniffed the bottom of the swing set pole. Corky then gave a sit response at the base the pole. I rewarded Corky at source. 4 Q tips of Birch on the picnic table and 2 Q tips of Bi at the base of the pole.

Figure 71 Example of a performance sheet

The Performance Diagram

In addition to the performance sheet you create a performance diagram of a completed search.

The diagram is a graphic depiction and corroboration of the information on the performance sheet. See Figure 72.

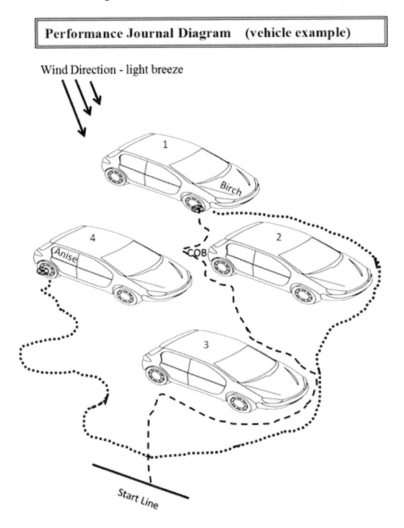

Figure 72 Example of a performance diagram

The Exercise Log

The exercise log documents the specifics of a training drill or a competition. The log tells you how many times your team has trained with an odor at a location, and how often. A nose work instructor can review your exercise log and performance sheets, and provide valuable feedback on your training regimen.

The following table shows you that in 2014 my team trained at the Tucson Training Center on April 7. My team worked two elements (vehicles and exteriors), and used birch and anise as the trained odors. We completed three events, which I documented on performance sheets 50, 51, and 52. Years later, I can review the specifics of the events by reading the performance sheets.

Date	Location	Element	Odor	Training	Trial	Exercise No.
4/7/14	Tucson Training Center	Vehicles Exteriors	Birch Anise	Yes		50, 51, 52
4/9/14	U-Haul Yard, Tucson	Interior Containers	Birch Anise	Yes		53 – 57
4/27/14	Santa Rosa, Ca	NW1 trial	Birch		Yes	58 – 61

Look at the row dated April 27, 2014. My team competed in a K9 Nose Work NW1 trial at Santa Rosa, California. I documented my team's experiences on performance sheets 58 through 61. I can review those performance sheets to develop future training goals, and read the sheets before another competition.

Chapter 7.
UNDERSTANDING HANDLER ERRORS

Handler error is verbal or physical communication by a handler that, when interpreted by the dog, causes the dog to manipulate the handler and/or fail to detect a trained odor.

This chapter discusses what I consider to be the most problematic handler errors:

- Poor leash-handling skills
- Poor presentation (detailing) skills
- Inability to read a change of behavior
- Conducting little or no search pattern
- Cueing or "telegraphing"
- Crowding the dog
- Focusing on one location
- Lack of knowledge of odor
- Lack of dog accountability
- Bias
- One-sided work
- Handler attitude

A regular, consistent training program helps to identify and correct handler errors.

Poor Leash-Handling Skills

The following table describes the most common leash-handling errors in novice handlers, and some suggested remedies.

Observation	Remedy
Handler is confused.	Develop a search plan.
Handler hesitates.	Understand how odor works.
Handler lacks confidence.	Perform leash-handling drills (see Chapter 3).
Handler corrects the dog with the leash.	Use a harness on the dog.
	Clip the leash to the dead ring on a martingale or slip collar so that the collar does not tighten.
	Work off-leash.
	Train with a few people to watch, then train in a big group. This helps you to overcome your nerves in working before an audience.
Handler steers the dog with the leash.	Use a harness on the dog.
	Work the dog on a 10- to 15-foot leash. Work away from the dog. Avoid distracting the dog with the leash.
Handler constantly tangles the leash, or tangles the dog in the leash (see Figures 73 and 74).	Use a shorter leash and train with different lengths of leash.
	Practice how to handle leashes (see Chapter 3).
	Perform leash-handling drills.

Figure 73 Example of a tangled leash

Figure 74 Another example of a tangled leash

Poor Presentation (Detailing) Skills

Presentation (detailing) is an art form. You are working as one with your dog. Over-detailing (moving a hand or finger multiple times in one area to pique your dog's interest) is a serious handler error (see Figures 75 and 76).

Figure 75 Over-detailing is a serious handler error

Figure 76 Another example of over-detailing

I've seen people point at the seam of a dresser drawer and expect their dog to follow along with their nose. The dog is responding to the handler's actions, not to the presence of odor. The dog will eventually manipulate you, or your actions will persuade the dog to give a false indication, causing you to misread your dog.

This problem is usually caused by inexperience, nervousness, poor training techniques, and a lack of confidence in the dog. Your goal is to present areas and remember who has the nose. You must learn to trust your dog. To correct this problem, present areas that might contain a trained odor. If you notice that the dog doesn't sniff an area you presented, or if you missed an area, present the area again or remember the location and present at the end of the search.

Inability to Read a Change of Behavior

A firm understanding of your dog's olfactory capabilities enables you to read your dog. So many handlers focus only on their dog when the dog has encountered a trained odor. It is equally important to learn how your dog uses its olfactory capabilities before it encounters a trained odor.

The ability to read your dog is formed by many hours of training and practice. Let someone else work your dog while you watch. Observe changes in behavior from a distance as the dog nears the location of the odor source. Search for odor in a darkened room. Listen for the change in sniffing behavior. Ask someone to film you performing a search. Review the video with your instructor, and watch your actions, not the dog's.

Work your dog in the presence of trained odor and distraction odors such as food, other animals, or dog urine on a tire. Note the differences in behavior. You will usually observe a difference in search intensity. Many dogs keep their mouths open while sniffing distraction odors but not while sniffing trained odors.

Little or No Search Pattern

Teams that use a search pattern tend to have successful searches. Successful searches depend on a consistent training program that reinforces the handler's confidence in leash work and reading the dog.

Search patterns conserve a dog's energy by using ambient air flow to assist in a search. Patterns also discourage you from over-detailing or cueing. Your dog remains interested in searching and isn't distracted.

Cueing

Cueing or "telegraphing" is a verbal or physical communication by a handler that is interpreted by a dog in a way that leads the dog to fail to detect a trained odor and to manipulate the handler.

Cueing is usually unconscious behavior. A handler may change the tone of their voice when the dog sniffs harder at an area. This teaches the dog that voice tone — not odor — is the key to a reward.

A body position, such as standing in one spot with a particular posture, indicates to the dog that your stance is the key to reward. See Figure 77.

Figure 77 Example of a body position cueing a dog

Ask someone to take a video of you performing a search. Is the dog telling you where the odor source is located? Are you focusing on areas? What is your body position as the dog inspects an area? Taking videos of your training sessions helps you to detect unconscious behaviors.

Crowding the Dog

This error occurs when you observe a change of behavior and move immediately behind or next to the dog. Because the dog associates your presence with being rewarded, and your body prevents the dog from moving, the only available action is to give an alert response, as in Figure 78.

Figure 78 Crowding a dog

One remedy would be to stay at the end of the leash until you are certain that the dog has displayed a change of behavior on a trained odor.

Use direct reward or pairing to reward the dog so that you stay at the end of the leash. Or, ask someone else to reward the dog so that you can remain at the end of the leash.

Focusing on One Location

This error is similar to over-detailing. You manipulate the dog to believe something exists at a spot that you repeatedly present.

Present an area once or twice — using a search pattern helps. If you catch yourself focusing on an area and the dog is showing an interest or change of behavior but you have doubts, move to another area. Search and then return to the original area. If a trained odor is present, you will notice a change of behavior and the dog will go to the source.

Lack of Knowledge of Odor

A novice handler poorly applies their dog because they lack a strong knowledge of odor.

When you train, be aware of the amount of odor that is used. Your dog's ability to work an odor problem may vary because of the amount of odor. Vary the amount of odor so that your dog learns how to find different amounts and experiences a variety of scent pictures, and so that you can observe your dog's behavior in different situations.

Lack of Dog Accountability

Lack of accountability occurs when a handler hasn't formulated a search plan and fails to identify searched areas and areas that still need to be searched. This problem can also occur when the dog is tired, distracted, or confused about the game.

A regular training program is critical to your team's performance. Train on the basic drills in Chapter 3 before introducing more complex searches.

Bias

This error occurs when the handler believes they know more about the odor picture than the dog.

During a search, the handler may be thinking *The instructor wouldn't hide odor there,* or *There is no way that the odor could be present in this area.* Preconceived ideas about odor lead to trouble, and ultimately plant the idea that your dog may be wrong.

When applied correctly, the dog will tell you where the odor is — and where it isn't.

Resolve this error with your training. Training helps you learn to read your dog by observing when the dog finds a scent cone for a blind hide. Ask someone to take videos of you performing a search.

One-Sided Work

This type of handler error can be attributed to a handler receiving inadequate basic instruction in working a detection dog. Contrast that handler with one who works their dog without intruding on the dog's pattern of searching and who assists the dog when necessary.

Working a detection dog requires a handler with the knowledge and humility to know when to assist their partner and when to allow their partner the freedom to use their olfactory talents.

Find an instructor or trainer who shares your training goals. Join a small group of dog enthusiasts who share your training goals and beliefs. Enjoy your training as a team.

Handler Attitude

Many of us who participate in personal or team sports understand the power of a winning attitude. Similarly, handling a detection dog requires a positive mentality at all times. If you have a negative attitude about your dog or your abilities as handler, that attitude travels down the leash to your dog.

Negative thoughts occur when we lack experience, confidence, or have memories of negative experiences. Some people do not know how to confront failure. Learn to accept failure as equal to success — a learning experience for both of you.

Your self-worth is not — and should not be — based on a positive or negative outcome when working your dog. Our quirky human traits sometimes lead us to undermine our dog's efforts.

Handling a detection dog is a game for the dog. Therefore, no matter your level in the detection dog field, you should be having fun too. Confront each odor problem with the attitude that it is a challenge.

Chapter 8.
RULES FOR NOSE WORK HANDLERS

Before every job, be sure to see your dog relieved at every tree.

Your dog cannot focus on the task at hand if they have to relieve themselves. Give your dog a "potty break" before and after each search. Giving your dog a potty break before a training session helps your dog to ignore areas in a search where other animals might have marked, and educates your dog when it is permissible to urinate.

The next two items for us to ascertain are wind direction and terrain.

Your task as handler is to determine the wind direction and environment before a search. Determining these two factors assists your dog in using the environment.

If necessary, ventilate the building before. Then close the windows and the door.

As you are creating your search plan and performing your safety check, you may notice elements of a building that can influence odor movement and your dog's ability to locate the source of an odor. When possible, manipulate the environment to help your dog.

A tired dog must be awakened
before a search is undertaken.

Allow your dog time to fully awaken from a nap between training sessions, and give your dog time to understand the search environment. Enabling your dog to spend a few moments focusing before the training session helps your dog to eagerly anticipate the game.

You alone will know whether free,
or on leash, the dog will go.

Working your dog on-leash or off-leash is dictated by dog safety or training criteria. Training to work on-leash and off-leash builds handler confidence — and handler confidence leads to a confident detection team.

Work thoroughly, and with care,
to detect every clue that is hidden there.

Handling a detection dog requires you to provide an opportunity for your dog to inspect an area. You must be thorough in your search routine and presentation.

Meanwhile, the handler (as we must)
constantly watches his dog with trust.

Trusting your dog does not always come easy to humans. But to become a good detection dog handler you must build your trust in your dog. If you train regularly trust will come.

It's a well-known fact:
Alone, man is inferior;
and the detection dog's search is,
by far, superior.

You are only half of the team. Let your dog use its nose to search. Don't use your logic to solve a scenting problem.

We help a little bit.
While, to our dog,
his wishes we submit.

Working your dog to a plan is a good idea. However, because your dog is identifying odor molecules with their nose, you must allow your dog the freedom to go to the source of the odor.

We must avoid standing on the dog's tail.
So, a distance behind, we will trail.

Give your dog room to work while finding the source of an odor. Have confidence in letting the dog work away from you. A handler that stays close to their dog will fail to properly read the dog.

We do not push, nor do we ask,
because neither help the dog do the task.

Continuously talking, and steering the dog with the leash, will distract a dog from detecting odors.

A handler who frequently gives his dog a rest helps keep him alert to do his best.

Be aware of your dog's physical abilities when working to detect an odor. Create extended search training that builds search stamina, but do not always work the dog at peak scenting stamina or to tiredness.

Dog loves this game shared with the master, and willingly searches thereafter.

Never forget that finding a source of an odor is a game for your dog! Have fun and enjoy the time together!

If he urgently points to what we search for, it's with praise we give him all the more.

Support your dog during the game. Offer praise to help your dog seek out the source of the odor. When they find the odor source, always offer boisterous and supportive praise with the reward.

And, if we find out our hardworking efforts were all in vain, then we neither worry nor kick up a fuss; but, reward him for efforts shown serving us.

Your team will sometimes experience unsuccessful searches. Don't display your displeasure. Praise your dog for searching so hard and for playing this game with you. Give them a hug!

He finds the toy that we prepared.
Only then lead him away from there.

Remember that this is just a game for your dog. Do not fail to reward your dog for a job well done. Be supportive by consistently providing a successful outcome at the end of a training session. End on a high note.

Chapter 9.
FURTHER READING

Bassham, Lanny R. *With Winning in Mind: The Mental Management System: An Olympic Champion's Success System.* Flower Mound, TX: Mental Management Systems, 2011.

Horowitz, Alexandra. *Being a Dog: Following the Dog into a World of Smell.* Waterville, ME: Thorndike Press, 2017.

Horowitz, Alexandra. *Inside of a Dog: What Dogs Think and Know.* London: Simon & Schuster, 2009.

Kvam, Anne Lill. *The Canine Kingdom of Scent: Fun Activities Using Your Dog's Natural Instincts.* Wenatchee, WA: Dogwise, 2012.

MacCartney, William. *Olfaction and Odours.* 1968.

Most, Konrad. *Training Dogs: A Manual.* Wenatchee, WA, U.S.A.: Dogwise Pub., 2001.

Pearsall, Milo, and Hugo Verbruggen. *Scent, Training to Track, Search, and Rescue.* Loveland, CO: Alpine Publications, 1982.

Stejskal, Susan M. *Death, Decomposition, and Detector Dogs: From Science to Scene.* Boca Raton: CRC Press, 2013.

Syrotuck, William G. *Scent and the Scenting Dog.* Mechanicsburg, PA: Barkleigh Productions, 2000.

Warren, Cat. *What the Dog Knows: The Science and Wonder of Working Dogs.* New York: Simon & Schuster, 2013.

REFERENCES

Craven, Brent A., Eric G. Paterson, Gary S. Settles, and Michael J. Lawson. "Development and Verification of a High-Fidelity Computational Fluid Dynamics Model of Canine Nasal Airflow." *Journal of Biomechanical Engineering* 131, no. 9 (2009): 091002. doi: 10.1115/1.3148202.

Lawson, M. J., B. A. Craven, E. G. Paterson, and G. S. Settles. "A Computational Study of Odorant Transport and Deposition in the Canine Nasal Cavity: Implications for Olfaction." *Chemical Senses* 37, no. 6 (04, 2012): 553-66. doi:10.1093/chemse/ bjs039.

Pearsall, Milo, and Hugo Verbruggen. *Scent, Training to Track, Search, and Rescue.* Loveland, CO: Alpine Publications, 1982.

Schoon, Adee, and Ruud Haak. *K9 Suspect Discrimination: Training and Practicing Scent Identification Line-ups.* Calgary: Detselig Enterprises, 2002.

Settles, Gary S. "Sniffers: Fluid-Dynamic Sampling for Olfactory Trace Detection in Nature and Homeland Security." *Journal of Fluids Engineering* 127, no. 2 (2005): 189. doi:10.1115/1.1891146.

Syrotuck, William G. *Scent and the Scenting Dog.* Rome, NY: Arner Publications, 1972.

GLOSSARY

Active sniffing

The process that occurs when a dog exhales through the midlateral slits at the side of the nose and pulls in new air for processing.

Alert

A response in the presence of an odor that a dog is trained to detect. A final response or indication.

Application area

An area that will be searched by a team.

Apply

To work a dog.

Area alert

What occurs when a dog exhibits an observable change of behavior that is characteristic of the dog and consistent with behavior changes in the past where trained odors have been present.

Blind search

A search conducted without any knowledge of how many hides or their placement.

Brachycephalic

A skull that is much broader than its length.

Change of behavior

"A characteristic pattern of behaviors, as interpreted by the handler, that occurs when the dog detects a trained odor. This differs from other olfactory interests that otherwise are exhibited by the dog in response to the daily environment ... the pattern of behavior may be unique to each dog." (SWGDOG)

What a handler must learn to recognize as associated with searching for a trained odor. Usually characterized by the dog displaying an intense interest, by tail flagging, intense sniffing with mouth closed, and sniffing (focused) on a general location.

Clear

A communication by a dog that no trained odor is present.

A room without trained odor.

Dead space

An area without the scent molecules of a trained odor although the odor is present.

Detailing

Also called *presenting* or *presentation*. A method of directing a dog to inspect a specific area.

Downwind

Away from and with the direction of wind or air movement.

Ethmoturbinates

Also called *nasal conchae*. These are thin, bony elements shaped like a scroll that form the upper chambers of the nasal cavities. Turbinates increase the surface area of nasal cavities to aid in the rapid warming and humidifying of air as it passes to the lungs. They are identified as *maxillo* (large) and *ethmo* (small).

Head snap

A dog quickly whips the head to one side or the other as the dog detects or enters a scent cone.

Jacobson's organ

Also known as the vomeronasal organ.

Maxilloturbinates

Also called *nasal conchae*. These are thin, bony elements shaped like a scroll that form the upper chambers of the nasal cavities. Turbinates increase the surface area of nasal cavities to aid in the rapid warming and humidifying of air as it passes to the lungs. They are identified as *maxillo* (large) and *ethmo* (small).

Odor

In this book, *odor* means odor molecules that are emanating or coming from a specific source.

Odor plume

Also called a *scent cone* or *odor cone*. A dispersion of odor in a given environment.

Olfaction

Smelling. For olfaction to occur there must be heat and moisture. Think of it as an equation: olfaction = moisture + heat.

Pairing

The process of using a treat along with a trained odor source. A treat is placed as close as possible to the odor source and accessible to the dog.

Pheromones

Chemical substances produced and released by animals that affect the behavior or physiology of others of its species.

Residual odor

The odor molecules that remain after the source of an odor is removed.

Scent cone

Also called an *odor cone* or *odor plume*. A dispersion of odor in a given environment.

Scent discrimination

The ability to find and identify a trained odor when other odors are present.

Scent picture

The combination of odors that are present when a detection dog identifies a trained odor.

Search pattern

A method of effectively covering an area while giving a dog an opportunity to inspect every part of the area.

Smell

A perception by the sense of olfaction mediated by the olfactory nerve. Everything that you and a dog can perceive by olfaction emits molecules.

Sniff

Perform a short, audible inhalation.

Tail flag

A behavior common in sporting dog breeds. The tail is held high over the back or moved vigorously in an unusual manner.

Trained odor

Also known as a *target odor*. An odor that a dog has been trained to detect.

Upwind

Toward and against the wind or the direction of air movement.

Vomeronasal organ

Also known as Jacobson's organ. A patch of chemoreception cells inside the main nasal chamber that detects heavy, moisture-borne odor molecules.

INDEX